1. **Woodside area of Meanwood c.1895.** Not one of the buildings other than the Parish Church and the house behind it still exists.

Contents

2. **Meanwood terminus c.1910.** 'Toast rack' bound for Elland Road Football Ground.

PREFACE

With a few notable exceptions the men of Meanwood in the early nineteenth century, mostly rough and uneducated, were employed locally as labourers in the corn-mill, tan-yards, paper-mills, quarries and on the few small farms. The processes of those days made the tanneries most unpleasant places and it is probable that this small village was regarded as one to be avoided.

In more recent times, for many Leeds people, Meanwood was that seemingly unimportant spot at the end of the tram track through which they had to pass on their way to Meanwood Woods, the Seven Arches, Verity's tea shop, Adel Crag and beyond.

A few years ago I decided to investigate the history of this little known part of Leeds; what a fascinating, arduous and never ending task it has proved to be.

W. A. H.

The upper reaches of the Meanwood Valley have engaged my attention for sometime–especially the early industry there, with its mills, tanneries and quarries. As a 'foreigner', therefore, I am delighted to collaborate with Arthur Hopwood in his story of Meanwood and its people.

F. P. C.

Many local inhabitants have generously shared with us their memories of village life–some going back to the beginning of the century. It seems right, therefore, to make a permanent record of their recollections and of our field-work before the evidence disappears for ever. We have also been privileged to look at deeds, documents and photographs in private hands which have been of invaluable assistance in our enquiries.

We wish to share our findings with the people of Meanwood who we hope will be interested in the details of life in their village in times past. The story generally relates to the period before 1939; due to lack of space there will inevitably be omissions which readers may find surprising. For these omissions and any mistakes we apologise.

We have deliberately included names of people and photographs of groups in the knowledge that some readers will recognise with pleasure members of their own family of former generations. Locked away in readers' minds there may be other stories or, 'up in the attic', there may be old diaries, correspondence or photographs. Has a painting or photograph survived of Scotland Mill or the big Meanwood quarry? We shall be pleased to hear from anyone who can supply further information.

So many friends have helped us with our Meanwood story that it would be impossible for them all to be thanked individually–nevertheless for their special contributions we must mention Mrs Derwas Chitty (née Mary Kitson Clark), Mrs A. Heap, Local History Librarian, Leeds City Libraries, Mr W. J. Connor, District Archivist, West Yorkshire Archive Service, Leeds, and Frank Rhodes and Alf Stead. We are pleased to acknowledge our use of the resources of Leeds City Reference Library, Thoresby Society, West Yorkshire Archive Service, Wakefield and Leeds, and Yorkshire Archaeological Society.

The generous help given by Mr A. J. Oates with original photographs 18, 21, 32, 33, 36, 38, 39 and 41, and the copying of numerous other pictures is gratefully acknowledged as is the assistance received from the University of Leeds, Audio-Visual Service. We wish to record our thanks for permission to include copies of photographs in the possession of Leeds Civic Trust: 12. Leeds City Reference Library: 11, 13, 24, 27, 34, 40, 42 and 44. Thoresby Society (Godfrey Bingley Collection): 1, 4, 5, 8, 28, 29 and 43. West Yorkshire Archive Service, Leeds: 15. Mesdames Derwas Chitty: 25 and 26. P. Cocksedge: 19 and 22. N. Crowther: 35. Miss D. Smithson: 17. Messrs P. R. Nickols: 6. F. Rhodes: 7. W. Shaw: 9. A. Stead: 23. G. Thwaites: 37. and H. Wilson: 20. and also for the reproduction of photographs taken by Messrs A. Clift: 16. and C. D. Hopwood: 14, 30 and 31.

Our thanks are due to Mr S. Burt for his advice, the Meanwood Village Association for encouragement and financial support and the West Yorkshire Metropolitan County Council for a grant towards the cost of publication.

If this booklet were to be dedicated to anyone it would have to be to the Beckett family, once of Meanwood Hall; the reader will find many references to their generosity to the local community. Their patronage was directed not only to prestigious benefactions such as the building and endowment of Meanwood Parish Church but also to humble purposes, for example the donation of £5 in 1886 by Miss Mary Beckett of Somerby Park, Gainsborough, towards clearing the debt of the Meanwood Parish Magazine fund.

W. Arthur Hopwood,
44, Parkside Crescent,
Leeds, LS6 4JU.

Frederic P. Casperson,
2, Wynford Rise,
Leeds, LS16 6HX.

1986.

Setting the Scene

Meanwood village to the north-west of Leeds lies roughly between Meanwood Park Hospital and the Meanwood Beck, and stretches from the Ring Road in the north as far south as Bentley at the foot of Woodhouse Ridge. Although the village is situated on the left bank of the beck in what was the ancient township of Chapel Allerton, the Meanwood story from time to time refers to the neighbouring township of Headingley-cum-Burley across the stream, and to the parish of Adel to the north.

It is commonly thought that the Meanwood Woods are named after the village of Meanwood. In fact the very opposite is the case. The word Meanwood is derived from the Old English (ge)mǣne wudu - 'The Common Wood', and so it must have acquired this name before the Norman Conquest. Around the year 1200, Thomas Peitevin confirmed a grant of land to the Abbot and monks of Kirkstall Abbey with the wood called 'Lemeenewude', and there is a reference to 'Wetwude' (Weetwood) about the same time. The use of the word 'Meanwood', in reference to the wood, occurred hundreds of years before it came to be applied to the settlement; in fact Meanwood did not come into use as a place name for the whole village until about 1847. Before then it applied to High Meanwood (Meanwood Hill Top) - the collection of habitations on Parkside Road. The houses in the valley centred on Green Road are in the area which was formerly known as Meanwoodside or just - Woodside.

Ancient Meanwood

All the countryside must have once been like the heavily wooded and boulder strewn Meanwood Woods and the terrain in the vicinity of the Seven Arches. The Anglian settlers of the Dark Ages began to tame the wilderness, felling the forests and clearing the brushwood, thus bringing the land under cultivation and establishing the field pattern which was to remain until the eighteenth and nineteenth centuries. They ignored 'The Meanwood', however, as the poor soil with its patches of overlay of glacial drift cannot have been very rewarding.

Some five hundred years earlier, however, the Roman army built a road from Ilkley to Tadcaster which crossed the Adel Beck near Golden Acre Park. There are also hints of a minor road and some defensive works near the junction of Parkside Road and Stonegate Road, to the south of the area once known as Hawcaster Rigg. From time to time Roman coins have been turned up locally, whether lost by careless soldiers with 'holes in their pockets' or hidden by fearful Romano-British inhabitants of the civilian settlement to the north of Adel Church, no-one can tell. As well as coins many other artefacts from this period have been found, namely: altars, pottery and brooches.

One wonders, too, where was the hut of the Iron Age sculptor of about the same period, who carved the Celtic head found near Stonegate Road. Did the same artist carve the 'Slavering Baby' (now so badly defaced) which is incorporated in the spring at Mill Fall, where the once popular Verity's tea house stood, or was it the work of David Verity, the Lane Fox's stonemason who lived there in the middle of the last century?

Even earlier than the Romans, in the dim forests of pre-history, Neolithic and Bronze Age men passed through the Meanwood valley. They left no major monuments, but they, too, were careless and from time to time their primitive implements have been unearthed. Examples are a polished stone axe (from Castle View, Stonegate Road), a fragment of an axe (Tongue Lane) and a flint borer (Tunnel How Hill), all being of the Neolithic period. The Bronze Age is represented by a flint knife (Alderton Place, Moortown Estate), a flint barbed and tanged arrow head (Miles Hill), and a large perforated stone axe-hammer (Spring Hill Quarry near the Seven Arches). All these and many other pre-Conquest artefacts are in the collections of the Leeds City Museum.

Middle Aged Meanwood - (twelfth to eighteenth century)

The 'Meanwood' lies in the old township of Chapel Allerton and in the middle ages the principal landholders hereabouts, under the de Lacys of Pontefract, were members of a family known as 'de Allerton'. 'Samson de Alretona' was granting land to Kirkstall Abbey in 1153, and in 1230 'William de Alreton' gave to the Abbey all the lands which he had in 'le Menewde'.

During the four centuries which elapsed between the acquisition of their estate in Chapel Allerton and 1539, when the Monastery, dedicated to the Virgin Mary, was supressed by Henry VIII, the monks had been busy developing and improving their property and receiving rents from tenants who were mainly farmers. The activity of the monks in the valley was not, however, restricted solely to agriculture; they worked the quarries, manufactured iron in their bloomery and owned a corn-mill 'on the water of allerton' for which a John Whalley was paying a rent of 40s. 8d. in 1540 when the assessors were valuing Kirkstall possessions. Highbury Works (Meanwood Tannery), once known as Wood Mill(s), stands on the site of this medieval mill.

At the Dissolution the Crown. took the Abbey lands, and in 1602 Elizabeth I sold Chapel Allerton - the Meanwood portion (i.e. roughly from Moortown to the beck, and from Grove Tannery to Sugarwell Hill) going to the old established local family of Marshall, with a share of the lordship of the manor. There were two branches of the family - Ralph Thoresby, the celebrated Leeds historian, referred to one as of the Upper House (could this have been Carr House?) and the other as of the Lower House (perhaps Alder Hill Cottages).

William Marshall (1591-1673) 'the elder', head of the Upper House, having no son, divided his property - some one hundred and five acres - among his four daughters by a Marriage Settlement of 1653. Later the estate was broken up and disposed of to members of the rising merchant class of Leeds, for example George Oates who bought Carr House (Carr Manor), and to lesser men.

In the late seventeenth century and throughout the eighteenth the valley was alive with small scale industrial activity, the water from the beck turning the numerous water-wheels for flax spinning, paper-making and tanning (grinding oak-bark), in addition to traditional corn milling. (These activities will be dealt with in more detail later.)

The population which up to then had been sparse was beginning to grow, stimulated by the opportunities offered by these embryo industries to both entrepreneur and workman as well as by the improvements in food production through better husbandry. Meanwood was, however, still a self-contained community with poor communications and the inhabitants lived and worked within its confines. One or two of the local notabilities, nevertheless, did have dealings with the wider world. The William Marshall mentioned above was an Alderman in 1651, and one can imagine him setting off on his horse for Leeds on Court days. Did he go by Chapel Allerton or by Headingley, for there was no Meanwood Road, or did he take a short cut via Bentley and up the Ridge by Batty Wood to Woodhouse?

During the nineteenth century some of the smaller enterprises began to falter but the valley was still widely known for its tanneries, one of the last major industrial developments coming in 1857 when Samuel Smith built his extensive Meanwood Tannery which alone supported something like one hundred families.

Young Meanwood - (nineteenth and twentieth centuries)

The first big step forward for the inhabitants of Meanwood must have been in the second quarter of the last century. Until then, unless one owned a horse, the only means of getting to Leeds for the villagers was on foot. The Sheepscar/Meanwood Turnpike dates from 1829, before which there was no Meanwood Road in the valley. Although steps had been taken to provide horse buses from 1847, it was not until 1878 that a cheap and more reliable means of transport became available. In that year horse tramcars began to ply from Leeds along Meanwood Road as far as Buslingthorpe Lane, and a timetable of 1891 shows that Coates's omnibuses provided a good service from The White Swan in Call Lane to Meanwood. Steam trams were introduced in 1898, electrification following in 1901, when Meanwood finally ceased to be a country village and assumed the role of a suburb.

Natural Resources

Land

Winning a livelihood from the soil had been the daily lot of the inhabitants of Meanwood from time immemorial. The higher and better drained land, albeit niggardly, did support some arable farming, but ploughing must have been difficult, if not impossible, in the gorge-like parts of the valley. The strict terms of the leases granted by landowners indicate their efforts to improve the fertility of these meagre soils. One of a number of conditions imposed by Sir Henry Charles Englefield, an absentee landlord, on his tenant at Weetwood Farm in 1806, was that at a specified time he must '... spread upon each and every acre of the demised lands when in fallow, three Chaldrons [about 100 bushels] of well burnt and unfallen lime or ten good Cart loads such as are usually drawn by three Horses of good manure ...'. There is nothing vague about the obligations of that tenant!

Stock raising and milk production were perhaps more suitable uses of the land. Deeds of the thirteenth century refer to both pasture and meadow, while in 1425 a William Scott claimed the right to graze twenty beasts between 'The milne callid mounkes milne unto Tonwaldhow [Wood Mill alias Meanwood Tannery to Tunnel How Hill or King Alfred's Castle] but if they escaped into the Abbot's wood called "Mene Wode" they were to frendly be driven oute.'

This pattern of husbandry had continued down the ages and although some arable is noted in the Tithe Award of 1844, grass predominated and by the early years of this century most of the Meanwood farms were producing milk for local delivery to the growing population.

An unusual crop, however, was harvested in the village. Rhubarb growing had spread up the valley from Buslingthorpe; the land now covered by a superstore on the site of the old Capitol Cinema and Ballroom was used for its cultivation until the early 1920s.

The number of hands engaged in farming began to decline about 1850 and agricultural land around the village was gradually sold for housing development. Meanwood Park (Meanwoodside), Meanwood Park Hospital (Meanwood Hall), Meanwood Woods ('The Meanwood') and the area around King Alfred's Castle are all that remain to keep green the memory of a past rural community.

Water

The potential of the Meanwood Beck (also known as Adel Beck and

Sheepscar Beck) had been tapped in medieval times. Adel and Headingley mills were mentioned in grants as early as 1170 and 1300 respectively. Around the year 1230 William, son of Alexander of Allerton, granted his mill and its pond to the Abbot of Kirkstall and it is on the site of this mill that Highbury Works, occupied by Robert Barker & Son (Fellmongers) Ltd, now stands.

The beck, which rises beyond Golden Acre and joins the river Aire at Crown Point Bridge, has been an administrative boundary since the Dark Ages, dividing the ancient townships of Headingley-cum-Burley from (Chapel) Allerton. In a lawsuit of 1560 the course of the stream in Meanwood was described by a witness as '... and so to Heddingleye More being also the Quenes [Elizabeth I] and there he ys called Woodmylne Beck, and so to one bridge called Monk Bridge and there ys called Bentleye Beck ...'.

In order to exploit the potential energy of the water a succession of goits was cut and some of the flow diverted into reservoirs from which it entered the mill-races to turn the water-wheels. Some of these man-made watercourses have been filled in but a very good example can be seen in Meanwood Park, running from the old Whalley Dam near Hustler's Row down to the Highbury Works dam.

To ensure a supply of water in times of drought, in 1825 the proprietors of the mills on the beck built a large reservoir known as Black Hill Dam (now Golden Acre) of twenty to twenty-five acres in area at the head of the stream. The *Leeds Mercury* on 18 July 1829 reported fully on a disastrous flood in the valley which, though no lives were lost, did much damage. Following torrential rain on Saturday 11 July, the water overflowed the embankment causing it to give way at midnight. Men at Adel Mill raised the alarm and '... communicated the intelligence to Messrs Andrews & Co. of Scotland Mill and Mr. David Smith of Smithy Flour Mill, who went on horseback to Leeds ...' warning mill owners of the danger. The bridge at Adel Mill was swept away and Stair Foot bridge almost demolished; Scotland Mill dam and Martin's Weetwood Mill goit-race were destroyed as were stocks of paper at Wood Mills and growing crops at Grove Mill. Properties lower down the valley also suffered - the total loss being estimated at £3,000. It took the torrent three hours to reach the river Aire.

Plans were afoot in 1853 to provide even more water, and Parliament passed a Bill authorising the building of two new reservoirs upstream from the Seven Arches. Nothing came of the scheme; the days of the water-wheel were passing and the steam engine was taking over. The revolution was gradual, however, and it was not until the 1920s that the last wheel in the valley (at Smithy Mills now Valley Farm) ceased to turn.

Landowners with water rights were very jealous of those rights and any interference with the flow caused immediate and strong reaction. When Eccup Reservoir was built in 1840 and enlarged a few years later, George

Lane Fox, Lord of the Manor of Alwoodley, pursued the Leeds Water Works Co. relentlessly for compensation on account of the reduced flow of King Lane Beck at Potter's Flax Mill just above the Seven Arches. This aqueduct, a substantial and well loved feature of the valley, which carried the Leeds water from the new Eccup Reservoir, is a monument to the then urgent need to provide the quickly growing population of the town with an adequate and wholesome supply in place of the existing source - the river Aire. The aqueduct was in use for only twenty-four years as demand quickly outstripped its capacity and an iron main was installed at the foot of the arches. This is still in use and can be seen at the level of the beck.

Edward Oates of Meanwoodside had water supply trouble, too, but in his case it was the behaviour of his neighbour, James Martin, paper-maker of Wood Mills. He 'stole' water by raising the level of the Whalley Dam by inserting boards (the grooves can still be seen) so directing a greater flow to his mill-dam which had the effect, not only of flooding Headingley Glebe land, but also of causing hides at the Whalley tannery to be washed away. Martin must have been a thorn in the flesh of Edward Oates and the adjacent riparian owners. In 1844 a series of confrontations occured and on one occasion Martin diverted the whole stream and Edward's entry in his diary on 13 April was 'Mr. Martin walking about like a maniac to all appearances.'

Wonder is sometimes expressed at the small size of the beck in relation to the work it was asked to do. One explanation is that it had a much greater flow before the Water Works Co. took so much water for Leeds; another, of considerably more significance, was the later spread of housing and the construction of roads and drains drawing off surface water which formerly would have found its way into the beck.

Stone

Not as romantic as 'The old mill by the stream', quarrying and dressing of stone was for long a staple industry of Meanwood and its environs. The Ordnance Survey map of 1847 marks no fewer than twenty quarries in the area, and the number of quarrymen and stonemasons, etc. accounted for more than a quarter of the employed people of the district in the middle years of the last century.

As with land and water the monks had the first word. The William of Allerton already mentioned gave to Kirkstall Abbey around the year 1250 'All the stone both upon and under the land which he has in Menewood ...', and a deed of 1257 makes reference to a quarry as well as to a mill and pond in 'Menewd versus Wetwod'.

The boundary fault of the Yorkshire coal field cuts across Meanwood Park, dividing the tough mill-stone grits to the north from the Coal Measure sandstones with their bands of fine clay, shales and thin coal seams to the south.

How these valuable resources - land, water and stone - were exploited is described in the following chapter.

10

Industry in the Valley

A passing reference has been made to the ancient mills in the area and it is now time to examine the various sites in some detail. Change of use over the years precludes their being collected into groups by occupation. As they are strung along the beck like beads on a necklace, however, they can most conveniently be dealt with by taking an imaginary stroll up the valley, looking at each in turn. Those readers who wish to make the journey on foot will find that, with the exception of the quarries, all the sites can be seen by the pedestrian, although some are private property - these are marked (P) after their name.

The route follows the Meanwood Valley Trail (leaflet from the Tourist Information Office) and is clearly way-marked by yellow arrows. The journey commences at Marsden's Monument on Woodhouse Moor and by way of Delph Lane reaches Woodhouse Ridge with a fine view across and up the valley.

At the foot of the Ridge across the beck was **Grove Mill**, a site now in the occupation of Messrs Bullus & Co. (Dyers) Ltd (P) and Yorkshire Switchgear & Engineering Co. Ltd (P). This is almost certainly where the medieval Headingley Mill stood. Doubt has been expressed as to the location of the mill but several medieval documents, an unusual divergence at this point of the township boundary, and the ancient names of the fields

3. **Meanwood Road from Woodhouse Ridge,** before the Meanwood Housing Estate was built, showing the Grove Mill site now occupied by T. Bullus & Co. Ltd and Yorkshire Switchgear & Engineering Co. Ltd.

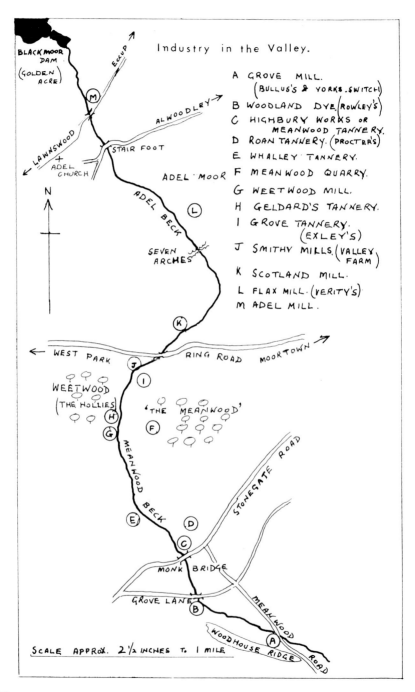

Industry in the Valley.

A GROVE MILL.
    (BULLUS'S & YORKS. SWITCH)
B WOODLAND DYE (ROWLEY'S)
C HIGHBURY WORKS OR
    MEANWOOD TANNERY.
D ROAN TANNERY. (PROCTER'S)
E WHALLEY TANNERY.
F MEANWOOD QUARRY.
G WEETWOOD MILL.
H GELDARD'S TANNERY.
I GROVE TANNERY.
    (EXLEY'S)
J SMITHY MILLS. (VALLEY FARM)
K SCOTLAND MILL.
L FLAX MILL. (VERITY'S)
M ADEL MILL.

BLACKMOOR DAM
(GOLDEN ACRE)

ECCUP

ALWOODLEY

LAWNSWOOD

ADEL CHURCH

STAIR FOOT

ADEL MOOR

N

ADEL BECK

SEVEN ARCHES

WEST PARK

RING ROAD

MOORTOWN

WEETWOOD
(THE HOLLIES)

'THE MEANWOOD'

MEANWOOD BECK

STONEGATE ROAD

MONK BRIDGE

GROVE LANE

MEANWOOD ROAD

WOODHOUSE RIDGE

SCALE APPROX. 2½ INCHES TO 1 MILE

(Far and Near Bentley) all point to this being the true place. There were many references in the early 1300s to 'Bentlay Milne which is called Heddinglay Milne' in grants to Kirkstall Abbey. No doubt it ground its corn for many a year while in the monks' hands but it seems to have fallen into disuse eventually as there is no clear reference to it in a rental of 1540.

After the dissolution of the monastery the land passed to the Saviles of Howley Hall and thence by marriage to the Cardigans (family name Brudenell) whose estate map of 1711 omits the mill. The potential water power was not likely to be wasted indefinitely and in 1797 'John Waddington, Gentleman, built a Cloth Mill and made a reservoir on Bentleys' (the ancient name of the fields). George Walker, yarn spinner, took over the lease in 1819. He was for a period in partnership with the father of Godfrey Bingley, the well known Leeds photographer at the turn of the last century, some of whose work appears in this booklet.

The substantial three storey building erected on this site, later to be known as Grove Mill, was subsequently occupied by Alderman Boothroyd (Mayor of Leeds in 1892) employing some sixty hands in the manufacture of carpet yarns. The site, which once contained three dams, was purchased by Tramway Supplies Ltd in 1919, the firm now known as Yorkshire Switchgear and Engineering Co. Ltd. Part of the Grove Mill estate was occupied by a John Naylor, dyer, as early as 1861 and two years later the dye-house was being used by a newcomer, Wilson Sharp, whose dwelling can be seen through the trees. This business passed to Messrs Bullus & Co. Ltd, the present occupants, in the late 1920s.

From the high ground near Batty Wood, at the end of the Ridge, there is an excellent view over Meanwood village. In the foreground, by the white footbridge, once stood **Woodland Dye Works** formerly known as Wood's or Rowley's Mill '... supposed to have been built about 1601 for grinding corn... It used to possess a fine old water-wheel but the wheel was recently removed to make way for the more modern steam engine. I can well recollect the time when the noise from the old homely wheel rumbled and echoed through the valley day and night.' So wrote 'E. J.' a correspondent of the *Leeds Mercury* in 1886. Godfrey Bingley's slide of 1888(?) catches a glimpse of this little old mill behind the cottages which huddled round it.

Whether or not the first date suggested is correct, there is no doubt that Benjamin Pullan, merchant, in 1792 was paying the Earl of Cardigan £60 per annum rent for '... three dwellings, Oil Mill [linseed], Stable &c and 13 acres of land.' Thomas Wood, corn and oil miller, and later his son, Jacob, followed but times were changing. In 1865 Benjamin Rowley, who was extracting ganister (a highly siliceous sandstone) from the adjacent quarry, took the lease and introduced steam power to crush the rock. The thriving Leeds engineering industry provided a ready market for the sand produced which was used in the manufacture of refractory bricks for furnace linings and for foundry work.

4. **Woodland Dye Works**

5. **Quarrymen at Rowley's** with Rev. W. L. Carter. (J. W. Holliday, foreman, marked x.)

14

Rowley purchased the property in 1890 (as an investment for his daughters) the premises then being partly occupied by Edward Crowther, a dyer. He founded a woollen dyeing business based on work from Morley woollen mills, from which locality he came, having eloped with the daughter of the principal of Mark Darnbrough & Son, brass founders of Drighlington.

Edward Crowther was successful in business and in 1906 was able to buy the mill and cottages. Thereafter three generations of Crowthers ran the business which in the end failed to survive the contraction in trade from Morley and the concentration of industry introduced in the 1939-45 war. The premises, not easily accessible and unsuitable for modern industrial operations, fell into disrepair and became derelict.

Leeds Corporation bought the property in 1974 and, after razing the buildings and filling in the dam, attractively landscaped the site.

Rowley's quarry was filled in after it closed down in 1916 and became the ground of Buslingthorpe Vale Rugby League Football Club in the 1920s. Some readers will remember the Coal Measures fossil tree which was shattered when the Leeds City Museum in Park Row was hit by a German bomb in 1943. It came from this quarry towards the end of the last century, and the quarrymen of the period appear in Bingley's photograph - the foreman, John William Holliday (marked x) is still remembered in the village. The formally clad figure is that of the Rev. W. L. Carter, Hon. Sec. of the Leeds Geological Association in the 1890s, who married Elizabeth Ann Rowley, younger daughter of Benjamin Rowley.

The path follows the margin of the old dam, and on the other side of the beck, beyond Grove Lane, was a field once known as the Bleach Grounds. A map of 1814 shows that one of the buildings then standing there was used as a bleach house in the occupation of a Mr Benyon (a name well known in the Leeds flax industry of the period). Later the tenants were Wm Hill & Son, linen manufacturers of Leeds and Weetwood, who used the premises for bleaching their products.

The route takes to the ginnel running beside the filled-in goit to Monk Bridge Road, beyond which lies **Highbury Works** or **Meanwood Tannery**, easily recognised by its tall chimney - for Meanwood village the most significant of all the industrial sites in the valley. This is the old **Wood Mill(s)**, a name derived from the ancient 'Meanwood', which no doubt once extended to its walls. As mentioned in 'Setting the Scene' it was granted to Kirkstall Abbey around the year 1230 and figures in numerous ancient charters, sometimes being referred to as 'the milne called mounkes milne'.

The monks had it for over three hundred years and, following the supression of the monasteries, it was in the hands of the Crown until 1602 when it was bought by the locally based Marshall family, together with a large acreage of land in the Meanwood/Moortown area and a share in the lordship of Chapel Allerton. The settlement of the estate of William Marshall (d. 1662) prompted a family quarrel. It was alleged that there were

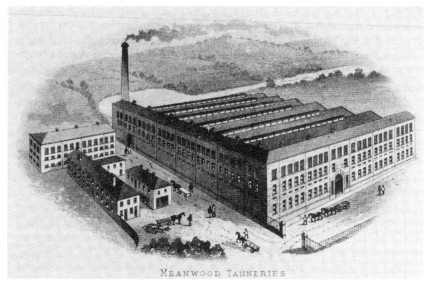

6. **Meanwood Tannery — 1891**

two wills - one spurious - but which was the genuine one? The number of possible beneficiaries was some twenty-four and as a result the estate was 'in Chancery' for almost twenty years. When the case was finally resolved the mill was sold and passed through the hands of successive absentee landlords who let the '... good Corn Mill, with two Water Wheels, three Pairs of Stones, a Kiln...'. The Garforths, Thomas and Peter, well known Leeds millers and corn merchants, were the tenants for some thirty years in the mid-eighteenth century during which period the mill was burned down.

A major change of use took place in 1785 when the lease was assigned to Thomas Martin, paper-maker. His need for an increased water supply was fulfilled by enlarging the mill pond; for this purpose an acre of the Headingley waste was enclosed for which Thomas paid a rent of five guineas per annum. This sum was earmarked for teaching the 'three Rs' to six poor children at Headingley School.

His son, James, took over the family paper-making business on the death of his father in 1806, and it was he with whom Edward Oates was at loggerheads over the quantity of water diverted from the beck. James died in 1850 but his son (also James), who had been in the business with his father, decided not to continue the family concern. After a brief occupation of part of the site by Wm Hill and Son, bleachers (of Weetwood Mill) the Wood Mills estate was offered for sale.

Samuel Smith, 'the younger' (1829-1880), tanner, was the purchaser in 1856 - the greater part of the premises being derelict after yet another fire.

He was the son of Samuel Smith, 'senior' (1797-1858), a well to do Leeds cattle dealer, butcher and property owner, who moved to Meanwood and took on the tenancy of the old Whalley tannery where his son commenced his career after apprenticeship with William Bulmer of Buslingthorpe. No doubt it was the father's money which enabled Samuel 'the younger' to acquire Wood Mills for £5,000 and build the massive premises standing there today. The carved 'S 1857 S' over the entrance archway and the enormous Meanwood stone lintel in an ancillary building should be noted.

When Samuel died in 1880, the tannery went to his sons, Samuel ('minimus') and William, the business being run by trustees during their minority.

The tannery, described in 1887 as 'one of the largest in the kingdom' and 'the chief support of the inhabitants of Meanwood', covered five acres with three hundred pits capable of holding seventy thousand hides - East India kips (hides of small beasts) especially being handled.

The Smith family association with tanning drew to a close at the end of the nineteenth century. The first Samuel ('senior') had set up his eldest son, John, as a brewer at Tadcaster in 1847 and in 1886 Samuel ('minimus') moved to Tadcaster, re-opening the 'Old Brewery' (home of Samuel Smith's Tadcaster Ales) which he had inherited from his uncle John. Of all the Meanwood worthies it is surely Samuel Smith's name which remains in daily and widespread use!

Harold Nickols, tanner and currier, was a tenant for a period before 1904; the premises then remained unoccupied until about 1910 when the brewer Samuel, listed in a local directory as a 'wholesale pork and pig-dealer', turned the tannery into a piggery. A good businessman he must have resented the fact that his property was yielding no rent, but the venture was soon killed off by an out-break of swine fever.

Wm Gibson & Son, fellmongers, and Meanwood Fellmongers Ltd were in 1914 in occupation of the premises, then known as Highbury Works, the latter company being taken over by Robert Jowitt & Sons Ltd in about 1920 when they purchased the property from Samuel Smith. In 1967 the property was bought by FMC Products Ltd, and is operated by Robert Barker & Son (Fellmongers) Ltd which company, as the name implies, continues the fellmongery use. A feature of the premises is a very large open ground floor plan where the operation takes place. Highbury Works is now believed to be one of the largest fellmongeries in Britain.

One of the earlier tanneries to be set up in Meanwood was **Procter's** later **Roan Tannery**. There is no need for a divergence from the trail as all evidence of the establishment disappeared on the development of the site as a shopping complex and small supermarket on the north side of Green Road. No details of the beginning of this venture have been traced, but it seems to have been established during the eighteenth century. Certainly a

7. **Workmen at Wm Gibson & Son,** fellmongers, before the first World War. Harry Smith on the left was reputed to have been a 'stern' foreman.

Nenian Procter (sometimes spelled Ninian Proctor) was participating in the local government of Chapel Allerton in 1789 when he countersigned the account of the Overseer of the Poor, which office he held in 1796. The township records for 1804 show that he was a tanner at Woodside with an apprentice but by the middle of the century the Procters had become quarry owners. From then on the premises passed through the hands of various owners and tenants, including the Smiths and Gibsons, culminating in Joseph Bateson & Son Ltd, tanners, who were at Roan Tannery from 1932 until 1966 when tanning finally ceased on this site.

After leaving Highbury Works the way passes through a gap in the boundary wall of Meanwood Park; formerly called Meanwoodside, the estate is described more fully later. On entering the park attractive newly built stone houses will at once be noticed across the beck. Constructed from the stones of the dilapidated Holmes's Farm and old tannery buildings, they stand on the site of the ancient **Whalley Tannery** (P). This was possibly the oldest tannery in the whole valley - certainly the first in Meanwood. Thomas Whalley, by his will dated 12 May 1656, left his 'Bark house [oak bark was the source of tannin] ... Tan house with the pits, to my sonne Thomas Whalley.', and the premises passed from father to son for over one hundred years until the death in 1784 of Francis Whalley, the last of his line to use the tannery. His will made provision for 'John Taylor [his foreman tanner?] to have the use of four pits in my Tan Yard during his natural life without paying any Rent.' Taylor lived for another thirty-six years! The rents of his Meanwoodside estate, Francis left to his grand-niece, Ann Rinder, after whose death the property was to go to her children.

The Rinders were absentee landlords for fifty years and when Edward Oates bought the estate in 1834 the premises were very run down. The occupant at that time was John Howson and, as already mentioned, the Smith family subsequently rented the tannery for several years.

It was then that the new owner, Edward Oates of Meanwoodside, began to have trouble with James Martin about water rights, although he knew before the purchase that Martin would be a difficult neighbour. Martin's rapacity for additional water supply prompted him to raise the level of the weir at the Whalley dam and byewashes (overflows), which resulted not only in the enlargement of his mill-pond at the expense of Headingley Glebe land but also increased the water level at the tannery so that '... skins placed in the pound below were floated away, and it was discontinued as a washing place.'

Three memorials to past owners are hereabouts. Built into the first bridge across the beck is a stone inscribed MDCCC̲ꭼꭼXXXIV - this was the former carriageway from Green Road to Hollin Lane. Between the beck and goit is a stone column; it came from the old Mill Hill Chapel, City Square, (Edward was secretary to the Building Committee of 1846) and bears a plaque recording the unstinted service given to Leeds by Edwin and Ina Kitson Clark, the last private owners of Meanwoodside. A grit-stone boulder with 'Francis Whalley 1723' carved on it stood nearby on the bank of the stream. This was removed to the Visitors' Centre in 1985 for preservation. Near the far end of the park is another column which also came from Mill Hill Chapel.

Across the parkland, on the right towards the north, the Meanwood Woods come into view. There lie the 'old quarry' and further into the wood the massive **Meanwood Quarry**. They may be inspected by making a short detour but little remains to suggest their importance or the activity which must have been the daily scene a hundred and fifty years or so ago. Stone from here was used in the construction of Holy Trinity Church, Boar Lane, in 1722, the present Mill Hill Chapel in 1848 and local buildings including Meanwood Parish Church and the Methodist Church. The Court House and Prison, which once stood in Park Row, was built in 1813 of stone from these quarries. The quality of Meanwood stone, however, enjoyed a national reputation and was used far from Meanwood - stone for the Royal Dockyards and the pier at Dover came from here.

The 'big' quarry, which was ultimately used for the extraction of sand until after the second World War, has now been filled in and only the top of the working face is visible.

Opposite Hustler's Row and the Whalley Dam (so necessary over the centuries for the supply of water to Wood Mills via the long goit) stood

Weetwood Mill (P). Now a market garden, this is the site of a small, late eighteenth century water-mill. From the late 1790s it was occupied by two generations of the Martin family, William (son of Thomas of Wood Mills) and his son Thomas - as paper-makers. They lived at the ancient Weetwood Farm nearby, and it was there, according to family tradition, that they would wine and dine the Excise man so well that while he slept they could purloin his official stamp and frank a good stock of paper to avoid payment of duty.

Although it was only a small country paper-mill it did not escape the labour troubles of the early nineteenth century. The *Leeds Mercury* reported on 14 January 1804 that five journeymen paper-makers were sentenced to two months hard labour in the Wakefield House of Correction for illegally combining to persuade and intimidate a man from being employed by William Martin of Headingley.

The Martins leased the premises from Sir Henry Charles Englefield, Bart but in 1858 Edward Oates purchased the property. He was particularly jealous of his water rights in the springs in Weetwood and in correspondence refers to '... the most delicate white paper formerly manufactured by Mr. Martin.' which depended on the purity of the water.

Wm Hill & Son, flax spinners and linen manufacturers of Leeds, followed the Martins in mid-century, using the premises as a bleach works, and Benjamin Grey, woollen printer, was the next tenant in 1870. His reputation as a very able dyer still lingers in the valley and it is related that if any nearby poor family suffered a bereavement he would dye a suit or coat black for a shilling.

The effluent from the dye house, however, killed the fish in the beck upsetting the then owner of the mill, Charles G. Oates of Meanwoodside, a nature lover devoted to the protection of animal life. With financial

8. **Weetwood Mill**

inducement he persuaded Grey to move his business away from Weetwood and the mill was allowed to fall down, but older local residents remember the remains of the pit and sluice for the water-wheel. All trace of this little industrial site has now gone, except for a stone arch over the tail-race where it emerges opposite Hustler's Row.

Ahead, the valley narrows to a gorge cut by the stream in the hard gritstone, and after crossing the beck by a wooden foot-bridge, the route lies between it and the remains of Weetwood Mill dam. Across the dam, where the stone houses now stand, was **Geldard's Tannery** (P). Nothing now remains, and little is known of this small country tannery. It is marked on an Englefield estate plan of 1758, but there is evidence of a Geldard (or Gelder), tanner, as early as 1728. The tannery eventually passed into the hands of John Howson (also at the Whalley tannery) and fell into disuse about the middle of the last century.

Towards the middle of the eighteenth century Geldard employed John Elley as a tanner's boy and it is said that often on wet Sunday afternoons he had to meet Mrs Geldard at Headingley Church with an umbrella and pair of pattens. He became engaged to Mary Ann Geldard, his master's daughter, but she died, after which he joined the army as a private trooper in The Blues rising, the story has it, through the rank of quartermaster to become a commissioned officer serving in the Peninsular War and at Waterloo. This romantic legend is well founded - Lt Gen. Sir John Elley, KCB, one time MP for Windsor, died in 1839 and was buried in St George's Chapel, Windsor - a far cry from an insignificant tannery in the Meanwood valley.

John Husler, the builder of the nearby terrace of twenty stone cottages - Hustler's Row (note the later introduction of the letter 't') and his son, Alfred, had a flourishing quarry and stone merchant's business in the middle of the last century based on the great quarries between here and Weetwood Lane. One, then known as Bateman Quarry, now public tennis courts, can be visited by making a detour into The Hollies but the adjacent Victoria Quarry is private. It is not surprising that the houses of Leeds magnates, professional men and merchants, who were in this period migrating from smoky Leeds to the Headingley and Weetwood areas, were built of stone from these quarries.

A third of a mile further upstream is a level 'table' of land, laid out as a picnic area. This was the 'filter-bed' of **Grove Tannery** or **Exley's Tannery**. Unlike Geldard's, the history of this little country tannery is well documented and the visitor will find plenty of evidence of activity here - stone tan-pits, the water-wheel pit and the small pond which provided the water supply for both the wheel and the processes.

Matthew Sawer, butcher of the Shambles, Leeds, obtained the land in 1801, the lease stipulating a rent of '... one Red Rose in the time of Roses if lawfully demanded.' (To get round what in the past was considered a difficulty in the transfer of ownership of land not in the possession of the purchaser, a method known as 'Lease and Release' was employed. A lease granting legal possession to the purchaser was made for a term of one year at a nominal consideration and rent. This was succeeded on the next day by a release, which in effect completed the conveyance of the freehold. The nominal rent stipulated in the 'fictional' lease was often one pepper corn, but in the present case the lawyer drafting the document had used a more romantic term - one Red Rose.)

Matthew built his tannery about the year 1814. Did the need to equip Wellington's army stimulate him? The meat consumption of a growing Leeds population and the locally abundant oak-bark (for tannin) would have provided a ready supply of raw materials. He seems to have climbed the social ladder quickly - directories of the period showing him first as a butcher, then a farmer, a tanner and ultimately as a 'gentleman'. He died in 1846 and the tannery was then let to William Jackson, tanner of Otley, whose son, William Lawies, would then have been about six years of age.

An elderly local resident tells the following story based on family tradition. The young Lawies, poorly dressed and wearing clogs, was often carried on her great-grandfather's back to school at Adel. Later his father went bankrupt and Lawies, then about seventeen years old, got the creditors together and asked for time to pull the business round when he would pay a pound in the pound. He succeeded and the creditors were so impressed that they subscribed for a silver salver on which their initials were engraved. At this time the Jacksons were at Grove Tannery but moved down to Buslingthorpe where one hundred men were eventually employed and later Lawies Jackson became Lord Allerton of Allerton Hall. The story teller's great-aunt, Mary Marshall, married Bob Tasker, Jackson's manager at Buslingthorpe, who was reputed to be a very able man.

9. **Grove Tannery (Exley's).** This is thought to be the only existing picture of the tannery. Meanwood Grove in the background.

Was this delightful tale of rags to riches another apochryphal story? Not a bit of it, the salient facts are confirmed by an entry in the *Dictionary of National Biography*, which adds that Jackson built up one of the largest tanning and currying concerns in the Kingdom, as well as becoming an MP and a Cabinet Minister. His son, Sir Francis Stanley Jackson, will be remembered as the celebrated cricketer and captain of Yorkshire.

Towards the end of the nineteenth century the premises were successively in the hands of a number of firms in the trade, but by 1871, George Glover and John Exley, employing twelve men, were the tenants and the tannery remained in the hands of the Exleys (father and son) first as tenants and finally as owners. It declined during the 1920s and was bought, along with the adjoining fields, by Leeds Corporation in 1926 for preservation as an open space.

Across Parkside Road at the bottom of 'Dunny Hill' in Adel Parish stands **Smithy Mills** (P) now re-named **Valley Farm.** The right of way is to the left of and <u>beyond</u> the buildings by a stile into the field on the far side of the beck.

It was occupied from the early eighteenth century as a corn mill by generations of a family of farmers and millers called Smith. John Smith, who was born at the mill and died there in 1853 in his ninety-eighth year, remembered going with his father to the '... horsing steps near Meanwood Mills to hear Mr Whitefield preach.' The obituary of Wm Farrar Smith (d. 1891) reported that his great-grandfather [John Smith] of Smithy Mills had lent his barn at Adel for Mr Wesley and Mr Whitefield to preach in. (The Rev. George Whitefield, pronounced 'Whitfield', ordained priest in 1739 was deeply involved in the evangelical revival of the eighteenth century and when '... forbidden to preach within consecrated walls he addressed tens of thousands without.')

The water-wheel was working well into the present century turning the millstone, and some of the older local people remember, as youngsters before the first World War, being sent to Inghams (the tenants at that time) for flour on baking day. Someone who recalls collecting 'sharps and bran for the chickens' in 1920-21 is certain the mill was in operation as late as the early 1930s and Mr Raper who took the farm in 1940 remembers the old mill-wheel being dismantled.

Does the history of this spot go back a lot further? Sir Robert Neville, who leased premises in Weetwood from Kirkstall Abbey in 1538 with permission to take wood for charcoal, made a will in 1542 leaving the 'Wetewode Smethes' to his wife, and it may be that this was the bloomery where the monks produced iron. The weir for the ancient goit, only recently filled in, was located on the beck just down stream from the 'cattle creep' under the Ring Road - a keen eye will spot the dressed stonework of the breached dam.

After only a few minutes walk a stone bridge is reached. This gave access

10. **Scotland Mill** after the 1906 fire.

to **Scotland Mill** which stood opposite, but only the remains of the stone retting pits (for soaking flax) and the unevenness of the valley floor are left to remind the passer-by that this is the place where a major technical breakthrough in flax spinning occurred. One of the newer mills in the valley, and not so important economically to the population of Meanwood as Highbury Works, Scotland Mill is of significance in the wider world. It is arguably the first place anywhere that the successful spinning of flax by water powered machinery was achieved.

James Whiteley, a Leeds dyer, leased '... a certain piece of waste ground adjoining Addle Beck' from Thomas Arthington, Lord of the Manor in 1785, for the purpose of '... erecting and building a Mill or Mills . . . for the Frizing of Cloth.' (Frizing was a process in the manufacture of woollen cloth.)

John Marshall, the son of a Leeds linen draper, had noted the immense profits which had been made by cotton-mill owners and realised that a fortune awaited whoever introduced machinery for spinning flax by water power. Marshall, an ambitious man, in partnership with his mother, Mary Marshall, and Samuel Fenton leased the mill from James Whiteley in 1788 and set about turning his dream into reality.

He employed millwrights to construct a massive water-wheel to drive the machinery he installed. Though a ruthless entrepreneur, he was no engineer and was in grave difficulty as a result of his failure to modify cotton spinning machinery to process flax. Help was at hand - legend has it that a young mechanic had tramped from Stockton-on-Tees looking for

11. Scotland Mill Cottages

employment and, penniless, had been given a night's lodging by the landlord of The Bay Horse Inn, who directed him to Marshall's Mill next morning. It was not the present Bay Horse but probably one of the old inns which formerly stood nearby. The young mechanic was Matthew Murray and he was taken on as a handyman but, appreciating his inventive skill, John Marshall soon set him to work on sorting out the technical difficulties.

Matthew solved the problem and his employer took out a patent on his behalf. Realising he was on the brink of a revolution in flax spinning and that he could never reap the full harvest at Scotland Mill, because of its isolated situation and the resultant cost of coal required for the new steam-engines, he moved his business in 1791 to Holbeck and there made his fortune.

Matthew Murray may have lodged at a local inn before he sent for his wife and moved into a cottage at Blackmoor. Romantics, however, will be disappointed to learn that his penniless arrival at Meanwood was unlikely; perhaps the truth is that the wily John Marshall 'poached' this brilliant young engineer from his employers, where he was gaining experience of flax spinning machinery, probably J. Kendrew of Darlington whose patent Marshall infringed!

John Moody Harrison of Woodhouse, a paper-maker, leased part of the premises in 1808 as a paper-mill but a year later the mill was 'consumed by fire'. Whiteley's sons who had meanwhile carried on a woollen spinning and milling business here were made bankrupt (had they fired the mill?). The Commissioners in Bankruptcy later let the premises to Andrews &

Moorhouse, flax dressers, and a number of flax spinners followed until the middle of the nineteenth century.

As with so many of the mills in the valley tenants changed and with them the trade carried on. The last page of the Scotland Mill story records the occupation by Edwin Ingham, bleacher, the end coming in 1906 when the mill was again gutted by fire, never to be re-occupied.

The path on the left of the stream accompanies the goit as far as the breached Scotland Mill dam, the finely dressed stones of which are very obvious. Across the stream beyond the Seven Arches stood a **Flax Mill** later the site of Verity's tea house. Nothing remains to identify the spot except the spring beside the path, which issues into a basin from a carved stone head (now badly defaced) known as the Slavering or Slabbering Baby. Mystery surrounds the whys and wherefores of this tiny enterprise - its workforce numbered only about eight young women. It was built by Miles Potter (according to local tradition without the ground landlord's permission) just before 1839 at the time when the Leeds Water Works Company's Eccup project was under consideration. It must have been obvious that the reduced flow of King Lane Beck would affect the water-wheel. When the inevitable happened Potter complained but George Lane Fox's agent, who obviously knew all about the mill, had little patience with him, remarking 'No sane man would ever have thought of erecting a mill [at Mill Fall] - and if poor Potter entered into a speculation which could only end in disappointment and loss we are not to blame.' The outcome was the construction of a narrow

12.   **Verity's** — once a popular refreshment spot for walkers and a well loved picnic area for Sunday School treats.

'cut' from Stair Foot bridge and a small mill-pond on that side of the King Lane Beck, both of which may still be seen.

The life of this little venture was brief, unlike that of the next and last mill in the valley, namely **Adel Mill** (P). The highest in the valley, this mill was situated below Adel Church at Adel Mill Farm on Eccup Lane. (The site is not on the Meanwood Valley Trail and there is no footpath to it along the beck from Stair Foot bridge.) Although not mentioned in Domesday Book it is referred to in a charter made before 1200 and a bitter dispute as to ownership, which raged between the Abbot of Kirkstall and the Prior of Holy Trinity Priory, York, for over half a century, was not settled until 1237.

Unlike the other old mills described, Adel Mill did not suffer a change of use with the passage of time. After a turbulent start its history seems to have been uneventful and it was quietly grinding corn from the thirteenth century until the end of the last century. The goit flowing from the old Adel Dam to the mill can still be traced and the wheel pit and fragments of the last water-wheel and much of the machinery have survived. (All these are on private property and are not open to the public but some of the old millstones can be seen in Adel churchyard.)

Almost a millennium has passed since our remote forebears began to exploit the potential of the stream and the nearby beds of stone. The present quiet beauty of the valley belies the bustle of activity and rumble of water-wheels which were for so long such important features of life there. It is now time to leave the industry of the valley and to consider other aspects of Meanwood life.

Key to places on map which are referred to in the text.

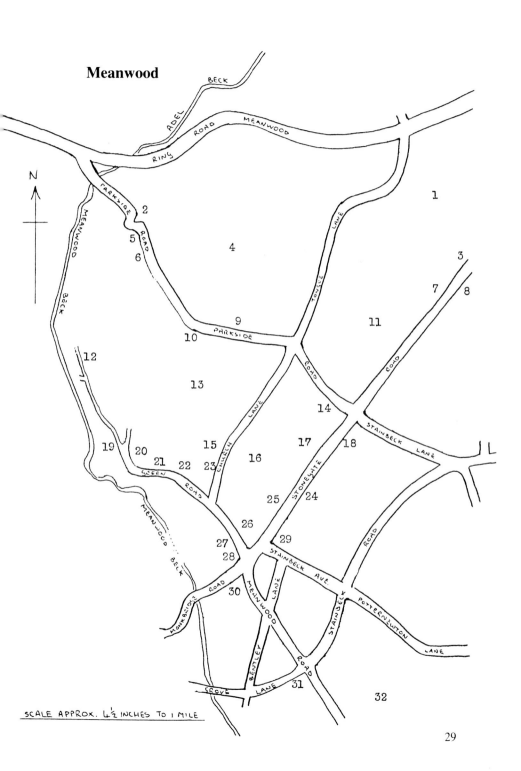

Meanwood

SCALE APPROX. 4½ INCHES TO 1 MILE

Church, Chapels, and Church School

Holy Trinity Church, Meanwood

When Walter Farquhar Hook became Vicar of Leeds in 1837 the parish was very extensive and included several chapelries of which Headingley and Chapel Allerton were two. He saw the need for greater pastoral care, and in 1844 his proposal that several new parishes be carved out of the mother parish was agreed by The Ecclesiastical Commissioners, the necessary Parliamentary Bill receiving Royal Assent the same year. Three years later parts of the Chapelries of Headingley and Chapel Allerton were detached to form the new Ecclesiastical District of Meanwood.

The *Leeds Intelligencer* of 13 October 1849 recorded that 'Meanwood Church has been founded and endowed by Miss Mary Beckett and Miss Elizabeth Beckett of Meanwood Park as a monument raised by sisterly affection to the memory of their deceased brother Christopher Beckett, Esq., whose unostentatious and practical benevolence and worth would long live in the recollection of the inhabitants of Leeds and who, having

13. **Holy Trinity Church.** Believed to be the architect's drawing preparatory to the building of the Church.

erected schools at Meanwood and secured to the district spiritual superintendence, intended also to erect a church had his life been spared to accomplish this work.'

Sir Thomas Beckett, Bart, who inherited the estate of his brother Christopher, wishing to fulfil Christopher's intention, conveyed to Her Majesty's Commissioners for Building New Churches, a field known as The Slade occupied by William Renton, on which the church was built and provided with its churchyard. He also conveyed to the Commissioners two fields as glebe land on one of which William Hardy's farmhouse and buildings once stood. They lay between the church and the present Church Lane; the first vicarage (demolished 1964) was erected thereon and the site is now occupied by Parkside Green. A way, two yards wide between the fields, was reserved to provide access to the church for all time for Sir Thomas and his sisters, Mary and Elizabeth. A footpath to the church was also provided from Green Road along the west side of Crabtree and Low Closes (Beckett land) on which the first houses in Church Avenue were later built.

William Railton of London was the architect, the general contractor being George Bridgart of Derby. The ornamental portions of the building were chiefly carved in London by skilled artists said to have been long accustomed to the architect's almost constant guidance. The two water colours on display in the Church by William Railton (who incidentally was the architect of Nelson's Column), very probably for the approval of the patrons, show his proposals for the interior of both the east and the west ends of the building. The style chosen was Lancet Gothic.

The foundation stone was laid on 20 May 1848 by William Beckett Denison, a nephew of the founders, and the Church was consecrated in the name of The Holy and Undivided Trinity on 6 October 1849. Mary and Elizabeth Beckett made a permanent endowment of £150 per annum and held the right of patronage which later passed to the Bishop of Ripon.

Maintenance for the sixth months to 31 December 1851 amounted to £20 0s. 11½d. which was paid to the Churchwardens, Thomas Midgley and T. H. Barker by the Misses Beckett, who when they died each left £375 for repairs and expenses.

Originally there was a ring of three bells cast at the Loughborough Foundry, the heaviest weighing 11 cwt, and above the bell chamber is the clock designed by Edmund Beckett Denison, later Lord Grimthorpe, also a nephew of the founders. He was a celebrated designer of clocks - the most famous of which is the clock of Westminster which controls Big Ben. The Meanwood clock which was built by E. J. Dent of London, has only three faces, presumably in the belief that as only open country lay to the east there would be no-one to see a face on that side. In 1885 one of the bells was recast and two more added. Mary Beckett, daughter of Sir Thomas, met the cost of the new bells and the necessary alterations to the belfry - nearly £300.

The south aisle was added in 1876 and during the alterations a marriage between John Bibby and Mary Marshall took place in the day school which was specially licensed by the Bishop. Six years later the chancel was enlarged and an archway made in the south wall leading to an organ chamber built in memory of Canon David Mapleton.

Other gifts by members of the Beckett family include the brass eagle lectern and painted glass windows at the east and the west ends. Windows were also dedicated to the memory of Thomas Wolryche Stansfeld and his wife Marion; Canon Mapleton and his son Hubert; and Major Walter Rowley and his wife Mary of Alder Hill.

Detached, at the east end of the churchyard, is the Beckett family vault, a stone structure being about fourteen feet square with a pyramidal stone tiled roof.

In 1930 a fund was started to provide a Parochial Hall, so badly needed for the rapidly growing community, and when £1,000 had been raised a site was chosen in the glebe on Church Lane. Lord Moynihan of Carr Manor laid the foundation stone on 25 May 1935 and the hall was officially opened by Lady Nussey, formerly Miss E. M. Cliff, daughter of Mr & Mrs D. Cliff of Meanwood Towers. To mark the occasion and to raise funds Eric E. Bullus published a booklet entitled *The Parish of Meanwood - A History of Holy Trinity Church 1849-1935*, the source of some of the above information.

Meanwood Methodist Church

It is not known when Methodism came to the village but the account book of the Leeds Methodist Circuit for 1768 records payments of 12s. 0d. a quarter from Woodside, the original name of the society.

Twelve years earlier Methodists were established in Woodhouse, and very probably their zeal extended to Meanwood. It may be that this development was encouraged by Thomas Garforth, a prosperous corn miller, of nearby Wood Mills (Highbury Works) and Scott Hall Mill. A prominent Leeds Methodist and local preacher, he built at his own expense a chapel in Woodhouse in 1769.

There were eleven members at Woodside in 1792 - Abraham Holmes, Robert Maude, William Maude, Ann Martin, William Waite, John Officer, Mary Officer, Joseph Winn, William Prince, Eleanor Groves and Ann Holmes. The earliest meetings were held in the homes of the members and later in the upstairs room of a barn in Back Fold, subsequently Providence Square, and now the site of Church Grove.

By 1811 the membership had increased to thirty-two, and in that year a plot of land on which to build a chapel was purchased for £5 0s. 0d. from James Martin, paper-maker of Wood Mills. The deed of conveyance states that the land '... as staked or bounded out with the house or chapel erecting and building thereon ...' was conveyed to trustees '... in the confidence that they would complete the building for use by people called Methodists.'

James Martin was the most generous subscriber with a donation of £21 0s 0d., in effect making the land a gift, and out of the £126 9s. 2d. collected, a Benjamin Midgley is recorded as contributing 2d. Samuel Prince, a class leader and stonemason, built the chapel, the first trustees being:

John Smith, Smithy Mills, Parish of Addle, Corn Miller
John Moody Harrison, Parish of Addle, Paper Maker
Ninean Procter, Kent House, Parish of Leeds, Tanner
William Martin, Headingley, Parish of Leeds, Paper Maker
John Officer, Woodside in the Township of Chapel Allerton, Tanner
Thomas Walker, Woodside in the Township of Chapel Allerton, Taylor
Thomas Watson, Woodside in the Township of Chapel Allerton, Farmer
Matthew Prince, Woodside in the Township of Chapel Allerton, Stone Mason
George Walker, Woodside in the Township of Chapel Allerton, Taylor
John Hardy, Woodside in the Township of Chapel Allerton, Labourer

Two years after the chapel was opened eighty-one seats had been let at a rent of 1s. 6d. each for half a year.

14. **Woodside Wesleyan Chapel — 1811**

By 1822 there was a Sunday School and an agreement dated 21 November 1831 reads:

'William Thompson agrees with John Smith to pay four guineas a year for the use of the Methodist Sunday School at Meanwood as a Day School; should any windows be broken, or any mischief done on the premises, he has to make all good; he is to keep the scholars from annoying Mr. Morris's house as much as possible; should the trustees think good for him to quit that he quit in three months notice. As witness our hands William Thompson, John Smith'

The Mr Morris mentioned, one of the seat holders and a local tanner, lived in a house very near to the chapel.

A Subscription and Collection made for Erecting Meanwood Chapel by Kenean Procter, John Smith, James Martin & John Morris in 1811 as follows.

Name	£	s	d
Mr. Kenean Procter	10	10	0
John Smith	8	8	0
Matth.w Saver	5	5	0
John Morris	5	5	0
Jas. Martin	21	0	0
J. W. Harrison	5	5	0
Jas. Brayshaw	5	5	0
Jas. Dickenson	5	5	0
Wm. Smith	2	0	0
John Officer	2	2	0
Robt. Slater	1	1	0
Rich.d Leak	3	0	0
Joseph Oates Esq.r	1	1	0
John Burrows	1	1	0
Wm. Burrows	1	1	0
Thos. Russel	1	1	0
Alexr. Cummimich	1	1	0
John Senior	1	1	0
Wm. Wright	1	1	0
Thos. Crompton	1	0	0
Thos. Midgley	1	1	0
Saml. Harksworth	1	1	0
J. L. Pipe	1	1	0
	85	16	0

15. First page of the **Chapel subscription list** with the names of the principal contributors; many figure prominently in the Meanwood story and will be found particularly in the industry section.

James Martin agreed to give further land to the chapel in 1849 for schoolrooms to be built, and two pencilled notes on the draft conveyance are of interest, namely: 'It is better to make it a purchase - Mr. Martin can present the trustees with a donation' and 'Are the schoolrooms already built? - Yes.' The purchase price is stated as £10 0s. 0d.

At the same time as the proposed purchase of the land it was agreed that new trustees be appointed, but neither their appointment nor the purchase of the additional land (on which the schoolrooms had already been built) was proceeded with, due no doubt to the death of James Martin on 20 January 1850.

New trustees were appointed in 1860, replacing trustees who had been appointed in 1827. The deed of their appointment refers to the land purchased in 1811, and then to 'Additional land acquired in the year eighteen hundred and ... ...', the day, month and year being left blank.

At a meeting of the new trustees in 1861 it was resolved that Mr Martin's son be requested to proceed with the sale of the land but without any result. Twenty years later the Superintendent Minister of the Headingley Wesleyan Methodist Circuit asked in a meeting, if the exact area of land belonging to the Meanwood Chapel could be established. By this time the name of the society had been changed from Woodside, first to Meanwoodside, and finally to Meanwood.

Although no conveyance of the additional land was completed, the statement in the 1860 document about it having been 'acquired' was accepted as proof of title when the property was sold to George Barber in 1883. Barber, a local man, would trust that the ownership of the additional land with its schoolrooms would never be disputed.

The building, with the date 1811 over the centre door, situated in Church Lane, was made into a laundry by Barber, a purpose for which it was used until about 1978, being bought by a firm of builders' merchants in 1979.

The trustees of the old chapel did not meet during the 1870s, but it was in that period that a decision was taken to build a larger chapel on a new site. Henry Harland, one of the Sunday School Superintendents, whose diary contains references to the bad behaviour of the scholars, particularly the boys, wrote on 15 April 1879 'A bazaar was held today in aid of the Meanwood Wesleyan Chapel Improvement Scheme - tea tickets 1s. 0d. each.'

The new chapel was built in 1881 at the junction of Monk Bridge Road and Green Road on land purchased by Samuel Smith in 1856, and it was believed at the time and stated in a leaflet thirty years later, that the land was given by him. This would not be surprising as Smith's father had been a Wesleyan Methodist and trustee of the 'Old Chapel' in Leeds, and his wife, Jane, was the daughter of John Craven of York, a distinguished civil engineer and prominent Wesleyan Methodist.

16. **Meanwood Methodist Church**

17. **James Craven's Class** on the steps of the Methodist Church c.1885.

Samuel Smith's death on 13 March 1880, one year and eight months before the land was conveyed, must have caused problems but the trustees were undeterred and construction went ahead. The foundation stones were laid on 2 July 1880, one by Samuel's daughter, the day's proceedings having commenced with a prayer meeting at five o'clock in the morning attended by forty-two people.

The conveyance completed in 1882 refers to a consideration of £235 4s. 0d. (not a nominal sum at that time). It may have been that a purchase price, based on the value of the land as included in Samuel Smith's estate, was inserted in the deed as a matter of form but never paid. Another possibility is that the trustees, most of whom were prominent Leeds businessmen, met the cost secretly out of their own pockets. The truth will never be known as the records relating to the building of the present chapel are lost.

The chapel was opened on 17 March 1881, the *Leeds Mercury* describing it as '... built in the Gothic style but somewhat modified to suit the requirements of the denomination.'

There were complaints that the new chapel had been built in the wrong place as it was away from most of the houses in the village. Seven years later, however, it was considered necessary to enlarge the building to provide a further one hundred and twenty seats and five additional vestries - the faith of the trustees had been justified.

The schoolroom and vestries, which are below the sanctuary, have been used over the years by many voluntary organisations including the Band of Hope, a Lodge of the Independent Order of Odd Fellows Manchester Unity Friendly Society, a branch of the National Deposit Friendly Society and The Royal British Legion.

Leeds City Council rented a room in 1905 as a public library, and the Leeds Babies Welcome Association (founded in 1912 by Mrs E. ('Ina') Kitson Clark of Meanwoodside) commenced to use the schoolroom in 1926 as a new centre to meet the needs of the Meanwood housing estate.

Meanwood Church of England School

When the Rinder family sold their estate in Meanwood, Christopher Beckett purchased one lot which included a field named Walker's Close at the far end of Green Road to the west of Tanner's Row (Tannery Square). On part of this land he built the school in 1840, which then consisted of the main hall, one classroom and the master's house. Christopher's charitable act is commemorated by a plaque beneath the belfry inscribed:

THIS SCHOOL
AND THE MASTER'S HOUSE
WERE BUILT BY
CHRISTOPHER BECKETT ESQre.
OF MEANWOOD PARK
IN THE YEAR OF OUR LORD
MDCCCXL

The school was in fact his personal property - he maintained it and paid the staff until his death in 1847. The 1841 census records Richard Kingston, schoolmaster, and Isabella Walker, schoolmistress, at Meanwood, probably the first teachers at the school.

In 1848 Sir Thomas Beckett, Bart and his sisters Mary and Elizabeth, conveyed the buildings to the Rev. George Urquhart, Incumbent of Meanwood, and his successors. The deed recites Christopher Beckett's intention to provide education for the children of the poor, resident in or near the village, and the wish of Sir Thomas and his sisters to perpetuate the benevolent design of the founder. The deed also refers to the gift of £1,000 made by Mary and Elizabeth, the income from which was to be used to provide the stipends of the staff and defray the expenses of maintenance and the cost of equipment. Provision was made for the school to be used on Sundays and also by adults.

18. **Church of England School**

The school was to be conducted according to the aims and designs of The Incorporated National Society and upon the principles of the Established Church, religious and moral instruction being under the sole direction of the incumbent.

William Beckett Denison became a trustee in 1864, the deed of appointment relating the deaths of Mary and Elizabeth who had each left £750 to the Meanwood National School Endowment Fund.

Eight years later Sir Thomas, under an Act authorising the Conveyance and Endowment of Sites for Schools, gave a further portion of Walker's Close on which the infants' school was built - very probably with financial assistance of the Beckett family.

Early in the 1870s Mr M. W. Nicholson was appointed headmaster, a post he held for about thirty-five years. He was responsible for many improvements in the lot of the villagers and was for a time a church warden.

By 1889 a further classroom was needed. An appeal was made to Miss Mary Beckett of Somerby Park, Gainsborough, a daughter of Sir Thomas, and she headed the subscription list with £50. The addition was completed in 1890 at the Green Road end of the infants' school leaving an outstanding debt of £70. Perhaps a further appeal was made to Miss Beckett for in October she is recorded as having given £100 and in the following month she came to Meanwood to present the infants' school prizes.

It is believed that a charge of twopence a week was made at that time, but one must wonder if it was collected in every case. The Elementary Education Act of 1891 was adopted by the Managers and thereafter attendance was free, but parents were asked to contribute six to ten shillings a year voluntarily. The Yorkshire Penny Bank introduced a scheme to encourage thrift and by 1892 sixty-four accounts had been opened by children attending the school.

A new cloakroom was built in 1892 and in 1912 the last major extension was made - the erection of an additional room above the classroom adjacent to the main hall.

The school log book for 1891 records that three girls had been transferred by the Waifs and Strays Society from the Meanwood Cottage Home to Mirfield. Attitudes had apparently changed by 1916 as there was then doubt as to the right or desirability of girls from the Beckett Home for Waifs and Strays attending the school. In that year the Rev. A. Powys, the vicar, received a letter from the Reformatory and Industrial Schools Department of the Home Office about the Beckett Home Industrial School and the attendance of younger children from such homes at local elementary schools. The letter went on 'If the managers of the school are unwilling for the little girls from the Beckett Home to attend their school it cannot be done but I am unable to see that little children who are resident at Beckett Home because their parents have neglected them, children under twelve, are in any way unfit to attend a local elementary school. Certainly it is infinitely better for them to do so in every way as it affords them more of the life of the ordinary child.' The letter then lists a number of schools throughout the country which children from local homes attended and goes on to say 'I have no wish to press the point but was and am desirous that the really progressive step taken by many schools should also be a feature of the Beckett Home School.'

This strongly worded letter, which surely did press the point, had the desired effect and many scholars between the wars will remember girls from the Beckett Home in their pinafores attending the school.

In 1922 Mr F. W. Cook, assistant master at St Mark's School, was appointed headmaster at Meanwood, and writing in the Parish Magazine on the occasion of the centenary of the Church in 1949 he said:

'Pursuing its course unobtrusively and with few outstanding events to mark its way, the School has played a not unimportant part in the Christian life of the village. Perhaps one or two memories may be of interest.

The even tenor of our way was once disturbed by an official visit of the Lord Mayor. It proved to be a very stimulating event. How the children worked to produce something worthy of His Worship's commendation. All enjoyed the occasion, and no one more thoroughly than Leeds' first citizen.

A Memorable day was that on which we were addressed by Commander Carpenter, V.C., of H.M.S. *Vindictive* and Zeebrugge fame. We were thrilled as we listened to a gallant naval hero and a very modest English gentleman.'

Many readers will recall that before the last war the school bell was rung twenty times at 8.50 a.m. and 1.20 p.m. as a warning that time for school was near, and also that during the war they took shelter in the cellars of Meanwoodside on the threat of air raids.

19. **Village Children**

Village Life

Little is known about the life of the ordinary people of Meanwood before the nineteenth century but the old Leeds Parish and Chapelry registers show that generally life was short, infant mortality high and the death of women in childbirth prevalent. Existence was a hard struggle, especially as much of the work available in the quarries, the tan-yards and on the farms would be affected by weather during the winter months.

The 1841 census reveals that for the area to the west of Stonegate Road, where the majority of the people lived, there were 144 houses occupied by 390 males and 344 females. Of the 233 men, women and young people in employment nearly all were in manual occupations.

There is evidence of poverty and ill health during the last century. In the Statement of Subscriptions and Disbursements for the Relief of the Poor in Chapel Allerton for 1820 is a reference to the payment of £1 11s. 6d. for the carriage of soup to Meanwood. The list of purchases includes 1,543 corves of coals, 3,897 lbs of beef for soup, 570 firkins of potatoes and 55 pairs of blankets. No indication is given of the localities of the Chapel Allerton township in which these items were distributed but some, no doubt, went to Meanwood. The names in the subscription list include Joseph Oates, Robert Denison, Christopher Beckett, William Beckett, Nenian Procter, John Morris, Joseph Lees, Matthew Sawer, Thomas Midgley, John Smith, James Martin, Thomas Waite and Benjamin Marshall - all familiar local names. They gave £31 6s. 0d. - a generous contribution for a sparsely populated area compared with the total township subscription of £144 12s. 0d.

Miss Anna M. Hellier, whose father had come to Wesley College, Headingley, as a tutor when it opened in 1868, in her description of Meanwood published in the *Methodist Magazine* in 1932 under the title 'In a Yorkshire Village' wrote, 'Meanwood, when I first knew it, was a quiet country village in the midst of green fields and far from any bus route. The villagers, untaught and uncared for, were notoriously rough, and drunkenness and immorality abounded. There, ancient customs still lingered, and the old folk remembered the days when it possessed neither church, chapel nor school.'

Dr T. C. Allbutt of Carr Manor, too, was concerned about the conditions of the local working class population. Writing in 1888 to Dr F. R. Lees of Meanwood, a renowned temperance advocate, he asked 'Can you not establish a crusade at Meanwood? I would most willingly give any aid in my power. It is an infamously drunken place, one of the worst I have ever come across, and it is at our own door that we ought to do something.' The biographer of Dr F. R. Lees commented 'The Meanwood labouring class were mostly tannery workers or stone quarrymen, physically robust, but of a low brutish type and there were then three public houses in the upper and lower village. Something had been done before by means of an Institute, Band of Hope and Good Templary Lodge, but only the younger end of the generation had been effectively reached.'

The Church School log book provides evidence of the social problems in the last quarter of the nineteenth century by its many references to the high level of absence due to illnesses including epidemics of measles, whooping cough and skin eruptions. Inadequate clothing and lack of boots and shoes were also reasons for non-attendance and in at least one instance the parents just did not consider that there was any point in their children going to school. Scholars were often kept at home to do domestic work, mostly before the Christmas and Easter holidays, and one boy was away from school for just over six months to look after his mother who was ill and his two younger brothers. The Meanwood Church burial records for the period 1849-1900 show that many children still died in infancy and that there were many deaths among young adults and among those in middle life.

There were, however, enlightened people living in Meanwood in the last century who were conscious of the plight of the villagers and by their efforts the following organisations and societies were formed to raise the standard of life of the inhabitants.

Meanwood Cricket Club

Between 1870 and 1939 there were numerous cricket and football clubs in Meanwood and up to the 1920s the fields of local farmers were in demand for pitches. Three cricket clubs have used their present grounds for many years, namely: Meanwood, Highbury and Woodhouse.

The Meanwood Cricket Club, one of the oldest in continuous existence in Leeds, was playing as early as 1870, the ground at that time is said to have been in the 'Poppy Fields' near Rowley's Quarry. The original records of the club have been lost, but some details of its history are contained in Meanwood Parish Church Magazines which have survived for the years 1885 and 1886 and from 1889 to 1898.

In May 1885 the members of the club expressed their thanks to W. T. Bolland, Esq. and R. W. Bower, Esq. for their kindness in permitting the club to play in Meanwood Park, the present grounds of Meanwood Park Hospital. They recorded with regret that Mr Bolland was leaving Meanwood for Scarborough, and that he and his family would be greatly missed for the interest they had all taken, not only in the cricket and football clubs, but in the Institute, day school, Sunday school and in anything connected with the welfare of the village.

In the following year Alderman Bower was thanked for having both the

20. **Meanwood Cricket Eleven** — winners, Leeds Second League 1928.

cricket and football grounds railed in with a substantial fence at his own expense, and the account concludes '... we trust that the players will show their gratitude by winning all their matches.'

On 12 September 1891 Meanwood played Leeds at Headingley and the record of the match includes '... our team succeeding in accomplishing the performance of defeating the premier club of the town on their own ground for the first time this season.'

The annual dinner of the club was held at The Beckett's Arms in 1891, the dinner being 'substantial and well appointed'. After the dinner, the President, Alderman Bower, made a short speech in which he referred to the very successful record of the first team and presented the prizes. During the proceedings 'A very handsome time-piece was presented to Mr. M. W. Nicholson, the club treasurer, as a memento of his twenty-one years service as a player with the club, and as an appreciation of what he had done during that period for cricket in Meanwood Village.'

The May 1892 magazine records 'The men of Meanwood who concluded last season with one of the best records in Yorkshire, are looking forward to the coming one with the most sanguine anticipations, notwithstanding that their match list must prove a trying one, including as it does the majority of the Leeds League Clubs, the two Pudsey organisations, Castleford, Wakefield, Ossett, Yeadon, Chickenley and the Shibden Hall Rovers, and T. Midgley and W. Fletcher are again to give their professional assistance.'

It was reported in October 1892 that the President, Alderman Bower, was then supporting the new Leeds Club and that '... we shall greatly miss the good cricket so often seen at Meanwood Park.' Meanwood Park, however, continued to be the home ground of the club until 1894 but with a less distinguished fixture list. A concert was held in the Church School in February 1895, the proceeds being used to defray the expenses at the new ground behind The Myrtle Tavern on which the club still plays. The magazine does not give any details of the arrangements leading up to the move from Meanwood Park, but as the new field was Beckett land, the family obviously helped the villagers of Meanwood once again, the club's use of the ground being rent free. The account for 4 May 1895 reads 'The first home fixture was played on this date, our opponents being Leeds Wanderers. This match practically opened our new ground and the wicket played very well and stood the test admirably.' To celebrate the occasion Meanwood won by nine wickets!

In May 1885 a concert was held to provide funds for a new 'tent' (pavilion) at Meanwood Park and for many years an old railway coach served as the pavilion at the present ground. In 1984 a new pavilion was built and a tea-room was under construction in 1985.

Meanwood Allotments, Parkside Road - formerly known as High Meanwood Allotments.

The system of dividing land into small plots to be held for cultivation by the poorer classes, at a small rent under The Allotments Act of 1887, was adopted by Leeds City Council in 1897. The Meanwood allotments were established some twenty years earlier on the south side of Parkside Road between the cricket ground and Fairfax.

M. W. Nicholson, who has already been mentioned in connection with the Church School, was deeply involved in the allotment project in collaboration with Mr W. Lawies Jackson (later Lord Allerton), tanner of Buslingthorpe and previously of Grove Tannery. Jackson was leasing a field called Copy Close from the Becketts, and his letter of 30 January 1877 to Nicholson reads: '... I have seen him [Mr Pollard, the agent] today and got a somewhat unwilling consent. I also asked him as to Rent. He says I ought to charge £4 per acre - I paying taxes as at present - of course I should only be able to let it to you on terms such as I have got it on and you would have to covenant to give up possession at any time without compensation.' Action followed quickly as Pollard advised Jackson on 17 February that the field contained two acres and twenty-three perches and two days later Jackson told Nicholson that the rent would be £8 10s. 0d. per annum.

A meeting of the tenants was held at the 'British Workman' (the Meanwood Institute building) on 20 February when the rules for the allotments were adopted. The original minute book contains details of the agreement with Jackson and states that the field was to be divided into eighteen plots and a ballot held to decide the allocation, the rent of the plots being fixed at 5s. 3d. per half year.

The first seventeen tenants were: John Watson, William Willows, John Mawson, Robert Richardson, William Walker, Joseph Pearson, James Roundhill, Joel Worth, Richard Shepherd, Matthew Wetherill, George Smith, George Moss, William Benson, Mark Wood, John Baker, William Lee and Thomas Clark, and the following year the total was made up by Robert Lacy.

The rules laid down that there was to be no cultivation or collection of vegetables on a Sunday, that the ground be cultivated with the spade, and that any tenant convicted of felony forfeit his plot immediately but with compensation for his growing crops. Yearly meetings of the committee dealt with such matters as the failure of plot holders to pay their rents, the prohibition of greenhouses, the problem of trespassers, and the consideration of tenders for vacant allotments.

Early committee minutes were written by Nicholson, but the following extract from the record of the 1888 meeting indicates that men were willing to accept responsibility in the community despite their being hampered by the poor educational facilities available in their youth.

> '... and the following rule was proposed that every tenant pay his rent every half year or give up his garding and not to let it go from one six months to another or the said garding be taken from them unless he be hill wen time be given by the comity but not to excede six months unless the whole of the tenants give him lieve.'

The produce of the allotments must have supplemented the diet of many poor families in Meanwood and there can be little doubt that the holders were involved in what appears to have been the major annual village event in the last quarter of the nineteenth century - the Meanwood Floral and Horticultural Show.

Meanwood Floral and Horticultural Show

This was the inspiration of Canon and Mrs Mapleton, the first show being held in 1874. With the exception of the year 1890 the event was held annually until 1902, and possibly until about the time of the outbreak of the first World War.

A minute book for the years 1897-1902 (the only one known to exist) gives a vivid account of the hard work put in by the show committee. After the show, which was always held in August, the committee met only occasionally until the following January when it was convened fortnightly and on show day. The cover of the minute book is inscribed 'MEANWOOD & DISTRICT FLORAL and HORTICULTURAL SHOW under the patronage of THE VICAR and THE LADIES and GENTLEMEN of MEANWOOD and DISTRICT'.

A general meeting in February 1897 appointed a committee consisting of

Messrs Norman, Wm Smith, Hunt, Bellwood, Nicholson, Scott, Turner, Hudson, J. T. Clapham, Dunbar, Hopwood, Groundwell, T. Bailes, C. Smith, Waite, Holliday, Renton, A. Wetherill, Whorley, J. Beck, H. Bailes, Parfitt, Maxwell and W. Littlewood. The show was to last for two days and was to include athletic sports and '... classes for horse showing and leaping.'

At the first meeting of the new committee it was proposed that the President be the Rev. A. Powys, Vicar of Meanwood, and that Sir James Kitson, Bart, MP, Wm Boothroyd, Esq. and J. J. Moseley, Esq. be Vice-Presidents. The committee then considered the area to which Class 111 - Meanwood Cottagers should apply, and on the recommendation of a sub-committee this was subsequently fixed as that within two miles of the village. Prizes ranging from 1s. 0d. to 10s. 6d. were to be awarded for the open classes and from 6d. to 5s. 0d. for the cottagers' classes.

One of the athletic events was a three miles club race - teams of five, the first three of each to count. The winners' prizes were three gold medals (value 15s. 0d. each) and the second and third teams' prizes were six silver medals (value 7s. 6d. each). £10 was agreed as the total of the prize money for the horse section.

A local farmer, Mr Shires, offered the use of two of his fields for the show at two guineas for the two days and this was accepted; Isaac Dunbar was to provide the refreshment stand for which he would be charged £4 10s. 0d. or £6 10s 0d. if he were to obtain a full licence. The band of the 2nd West Yorkshire Volunteer Engineers was engaged for the two days, the fee for twenty performers being 13s. 0d. each and £1 6s. 0d. for the bandmaster; a wagonette was to be hired to transport the band to the show.

George Brotherton was asked to obtain advertising for the one thousand schedules that were to be printed, and he was to receive a quarter of the amount collected '... provided that the money be paid to the society not later than 10 August next.' Six hundred programmes were obtained for the sports events, and included in the payments made by the treasurer were: J. S. Saville, printing £21 4s. 0d., J. Hobson, joinery £4 10s. 0d., two night watchmen 10s. 0d. each, Mr Gibbs, rosettes £1 10s. 0d., Police £2 8s. 0d. and handicappers £1 1s. 0d.

The committee agreed to have a dinner on Thursday, 2 September at 7.00 p.m. at The Beckett's Arms at 2s. 6d. each, '... everyone to pay for what they order after the dinner cloth was removed.'

The *Yorkshire Post* and *Leeds Mercury* gave very full accounts of the show, and in the list of prize winners in the horse section there were entries from as far afield as Hipperholme, Knaresborough, Boroughbridge and Alford, Lincolnshire. A further indication of the show's importance may be gained from the fact that two years previously the total prize money was £120.

The show was on one day only in 1898 and at a special general meeting held in April of that year it was resolved 'That having regard to the strong expression of opinion by the President and others in favour of abolishing the sports, that this meeting decides to try for one year a show without foot races or similar sports.' The reason given was that 'The foot races have been the occasion of betting and gambling and other most objectionable features and have done harm to the show.'

A special committee meeting was held on the Monday following this show to settle an objection raised by a Mr Eden against another competitor who had been awarded the first prize for black currants and eschalots, both parties being invited to the meeting. It had also been agreed the previous Saturday that three members of the committee call and inspect the garden of the prize winner to ascertain if he did grow black currants and eschalots. The record of the Monday meeting tells its own story - Eden had his 5s. 0d. returned (his objection fee) and was awarded the first prize for his black currants and eschalots. The other competitor had 5s. 0d. deducted from his prize money and was prohibited from exhibiting at any future show of the society!

Athletics were re-introduced next year, the main events and prize money for the winners being for the 100 yards - £4 4s. 0d., for the 440 yards and 880 yards - each £3 3s. 0d. The admission charges for the show were: Friday 2.00 p.m. to 4.00 p.m. 1s. 0d., 4.00 p.m. to close 6d., marquee for dancing 3d., Saturday all day 6d., children half price, vehicles 6d. per wheel.

Something went wrong in 1899, but what is not recorded in the minutes - was it the re-introduction of the athletic sports? At a meeting held on 1 February 1900 it was resolved that there be a show that year and arrangements be put in hand. The record of the meeting held a month later, however, reveals disagreement. There is the usual statement about the minutes of the last meeting having been read and confirmed, but either then or later the word 'confirmed' was crossed out. There follows 'A letter was then read from Mr. J. T. Clapham announcing his resignation from Treasurership and Committee.' After some discussion it was resolved that 'This meeting be adjourned until Thursday the 8 March and that it be then decided whether the show be carried on or not.'

At the adjourned meeting Clapham's resignation was accepted and another treasurer appointed. It was then resolved, but the minutes do not state why, that the seventeen members of the committee present sign the minute book which they did. Although there is no resolution that the show be continued it was nevertheless resolved that Saville do all the printing! Subsequent minutes confirm that the organisation did continue, the name being changed to 'The Meanwood Horticultural Society'. The date and circumstances of the end of this annual event are not known as later minute books have not survived.

Meanwood Institute, Green Road

The Institute is an early example of the Beckett family's concern for the people of Meanwood. William Beckett purchased land on which the Institute stands in 1810 but when and by whom the building was erected is unknown. It would, however, appear to date from early in the nineteenth century.

A 'public house without the drink' was opened in Leeds in 1867, the first of many such establishments in the city and throughout the country. They were temperance meeting houses with a religious emphasis, all becoming known as 'British Workman'. There was a British Workman in Meanwood in 1876, a directory of 1882 showing it as being in the Institute building.

21. **Meanwood Institute**

By 1885 the premises had become the Meanwood Institute which in January of that year received the sum of £16 18s. 10d., part of the profit of the Meanwood Fine Art Exhibition. Also in that year Sir Edmund Beckett Denison agreed to the addition of a room for billiards and Mr Bradley, tenant of the adjacent field, allowed the use of 'A strip of land at the back in order that coals might be delivered more easily.' The accounts for the following year show that the building work by J. Hobson cost £57 10s. 8d. and the fitting up of the new billiard-room £5 5s. 4d. Receipts totalled £12 2s 5d. which sum included a donation by Miss Mary Beckett who added a further £6 3s. 3d. to defray the cost of the furnishings.

A new full size billiard-table by Mawson of Leeds was installed three years later and it is interesting to note that after almost a century it is still in use. Local and national newspapers were provided together with other publications and there was a small but useful library. Subscriptions to the Institute were 6d. per month, a game of billiards costing 2d.

The officers and committee for 1892 were: President, the Vicar, Vice-Presidents, J. Bower, R. W. Bower, Rev. J. Buchanan, J. W. Heeles, C. G. Oates and F. Walker, and the committee W. Barber, G. Barber, B. Dacre, J. Exley, J. Elsworth, J. Hobson, C. Ingle, T. Jordan, A. P. Nicholson, M. W. Nicholson, J. Ramsden (Secretary), F. Wood (Treasurer), and F. W. Holland (Librarian).

In 1939 the Rt Hon. Ralph William Ernest Beckett, Third Baron Grimthorpe, and trustees, sold to Ernest Haley the land on which he built the Sunset estate. The Institute stood in the south-west corner of this land and in 1940 Haley sold it to Trustees for £100, at the same time advancing them that sum, no doubt to facilitate the purchase. No interest was to be charged if the loan was repaid by 1 October 1943 after which it was to be at the rate of four per cent per annum. Haley's nephew, Brian Haley, has always understood that his uncle gave the building to Meanwood and this would appear to be true as there is no record in the Institute accounts of the loan having been repaid.

* * * * *

New social activities sprang up in the early days of the present century of which the following are to be noted.

A Women's Institute was established in 1919, normally a rural activity, and indicative of the village atmosphere of that day. Meetings were held in various buildings but the need for a permanent home was always recognised. Towards that end a building fund was opened, and in 1934 the committee was able to draw up plans for its own Institute Hall. Lt Col Kitson Clark offered the members a piece of ground in Meanwoodside at the nominal rent of one shilling per year, and the new hall was formally opened on 19 March 1935 by Mrs Edward Shaw, President of the County Federation of Women's Institutes.

Following the very large increase in the local population, as a direct result of the new Meanwood Housing Estate, the Meanwood Working Men's Club formed in 1905 which met in the Liberal Club building in Stonegate Road, increased its membership and in 1923 built new premises. About nine years later the building was extended, the new concert room being called The Rodilli - a name chosen by a member because 'the road was hilly' - a story confirmed by a very reliable source. The present membership of the club is about two thousand five hundred.

Another village amenity, the Capitol Cinema on Green Road, was built in

22. **Liberal Club outing July 1909,** using one of Robert Barr's omnibuses. Old Beckett's Arms in background on right.

1922, the name being chosen by a local resident, and the *Leeds Mercury* account of the opening by the Lord Mayor includes '... it will be accepted as a boon by the many neglected people residing in the Meanwood district.' It met with immediate success, particularly the Saturday matinée - better known as 'the twopenny rush'. The ballroom followed and drew dancing enthusiasts from all over Yorkshire, and in the 1930s there was a café and also six billiard tables in the cinema part of the building. However, by 1968 times had changed - the cinema was converted into a bingo hall and the ballroom, said in the 1940s and '50s to have been 'the dictator of fashion', became a night club - 'The Cat's Whiskers'. This was not a successful venture and it shut its doors in 1978, the bingo hall closing in the following year. The final act came in 1980 when the buildings were demolished, but for thousands of Yorkshire folk memories of good times at the 'Cap' still linger on. A superstore was built on the site in 1984 to meet the needs of the area.

A further development was the introduction of activities for young people. The 2nd Leeds Company of The Boys' Brigade was formed in 1892, the Captain being Mr T. A. Hall. It ceased to meet about 1910 by which time the 9th North West Leeds Scout Troop had been established in the village with Mr A. Shoesmith as its Scoutmaster. The troop's first headquarters was the cellar of a house in Greenwood Mount, but after a short while it moved to a cottage in the grounds of Meanwoodside. One member of this troop in those early years remembers helping Col Kitson Clark to place some of the grind-stones still to be seen in the beck. He also recollects that during the first World War scouts over sixteen were asked to volunteer for special service and members of the Meanwood troop helped the police to guard Swinsty Reservoir in the Washburn Valley. Both leaders were called up for military service and the troop was disbanded during the war years.

Between the wars there was for a period another Boys' Brigade Company and units of the Guide and Scout Associations were formed at the Church and Chapel respectively; these serve the community to the present day.

*　*　*　*　*

Of wider application were:

Beckett Home and Meanwood Cottage Home

The Meanwood Parish Magazine for January 1885 published an appeal from the Church of England Central Society for the Protection of Waifs and Strays pointing out the plight of many children in London and other large towns about which the Church of England had done so little. Perhaps as a direct result of this appeal, a meeting was held on 24 February 1885 in the rooms of the Mayor of Leeds, which was addressed by the Rev. T. G. Butterworth of Meanwood, Honorary Secretary of the Ripon Diocese. It was then agreed that a public meeting be held to consider the possibility of providing a home for waifs and strays.

By September of that year arrangements were in hand for the purchase of part of a field between Brick Row and Hutton's Buildings, Meanwood, on which a home was to be built for twenty-five young girls, the first such home to be built in the Diocese. It was to be a certified Industrial School and a government grant would be paid for each child admitted. (Industrial Schools were established under an Act of 1861 to care for children in need, to provide education and to teach them a trade - most probably domestic work in this case.) The Diocesan Committee pledged £100 a year and the Central Society agreed to meet the cost of the home in excess of these two sources of income. There was £1,619 in the Diocesan fund, of which Miss Mary Beckett of Somerby Park had contributed £700.

Although a brick building had been planned, numerous householders in the village signed a petition asking Miss Beckett to use her influence with the committee to have the building faced with stone. Miss Beckett, who had already given a further £300, not only supported the villagers but also agreed to pay the additional cost involved - £200. The magazine in acknowledging this generosity remarked that it would provide work for the quarrymen and stonemasons living in their midst.

A delay in starting the building was caused by the Government Inspector disagreeing with one or two matters, but it was reported in May 1886 that, if Leeds Corporation approved revised plans, an early start would be made. The Corporation must have been co-operative as a carved stone over the door bears the date 1886 and, although the actual opening date is not known, twenty-eight girls were in residence by 1889.

Many gifts were received by the home, especially food and clothing, a very interesting present being two dozen spoons from Baroness Schimmelpenninck Van Der Oije Nijenbeek of Holland. In 1895 Miss Beckett gave a further £100 towards the cost of a new laundry.

Being an Industrial School the home had to be visited by one of Her Majesty's Inspectors of Reformatory and Industrial Schools, and the report following a visit in 1891 reads:

> 'I have today inspected the school and have found all going well. The premises are beautifully clean and neat. I found the girls looking very well and they passed a very good examination in the schoolroom where they were very quiet and orderly. The school seems very well managed. I have been much pleased with my visit.'

The home, still for waifs and strays, was converted into a nursery for thirty babies in 1935, the formal opening being performed by Lord Grimthorpe. Twenty years later the Beckett Nursery, as it was then known, had become the responsibility of Leeds Corporation. Subsequently the original building and later extensions were sold and converted into flats. Houses and flats have also been built in what used to be the orchard and garden between the home and Greenwood Mount.

Another home for waifs and strays, The Meanwood Cottage Home, had been established on the south side of Green Road, most probably in Meanwood Grange, owned by Messrs Samuel and William Smith of the tannery. Accommodating ten girls, it existed for only about two years, for in January 1891 the Parish Magazine announced its transfer to St Agnes Home, Mirfield. The Ripon Diocesan Committee thought it would be better not to have three homes quite so close together - the third being St Chad's House, Far Headingley.

Convalescent Home For Children, Stonegate Road

A Leeds Directory for 1882-83 states under Meanwood 'Here also is one of those unostentatious private charities for the benefit of the young which always excite the warmest sympathy and admiration - viz. a Convalescent Home for Children between the ages of three and twelve years. It was built by Mrs. Mapleton the wife of the vicar [Rev. D. Mapleton] the site being given by Miss Beckett. The Home is supported by voluntary contributions.'

According to the Rules of Management the home, which was built in 1879, was for the benefit of poor children. In addition to a further gift of land in 1883 Mary Beckett contributed £1,111 19s. 0d. towards its construction and maintenance and subsequently a legacy of £750 was received from the estate of the Hon. Mrs Beckett.

Children could be nominated for admission to the home by those making annual contributions, the larger the gift the higher the number of allowed nominations. A stay of three weeks was free but for extended periods up to a maximum of a further three weeks a charge of 8s. 0d. per week was made.

Towards the end of the century about two hundred and twenty children were admitted each year and in 1893 well over half were suffering from debility and twelve of the others were said to have had typhoid.

The home received a 'windfall' in 1896 - a legacy of £3,000 under the will of Thomas Turner of Gipton - which allowed alterations and improvements to be made to the premises.

Between 1941 and 1947 the home, adjacent to the playing fields on the west side of Stonegate Road, was closed and the building converted into flats about 1950.

Meanwood Hall, Meanwoodside, and Carr Manor

Meanwood Hall now Meanwood Park Hospital and the Denison and Beckett Families

In 1762 Thomas Denison (1720-1769) of Leeds, purchased a dwellinghouse and thirteen acres at 'Mesnewood [sic] otherwise Hawcaster Rigg in Chapel Allerton ...' and there built his home - Meanwood Hall.

Thomas died in France leaving his estate to his wife, Elizabeth, for life and then to his son, Robert. Elizabeth vacated the Hall shortly after her husband's death when it was described in an advertisement in the *Leeds Intelligencer* as containing 'Four spacious rooms on the ground floor, with very good bedrooms over, kitchen, pantries, servants' hall, coachhouse, stabling for ten horses and about twenty acres of land.' For some years the estate was let - the various tenants including Thomas Turton, the Countess of Aberdeen, Sir John Beckett (who owned two adjacent cottages) and Joseph Lees respectively.

The Becketts came originally from Barnsley and it was the tenancy of Sir John (1743-1826), a banker, who later lived at Gledhow Hall, that forged the

23. **Meanwood Hall:** pre-hospital days.

first link in the family's association with Meanwood which was to last for over a hundred years. Sir John's son, Christopher, also a banker, bought the property from Robert Denison in 1824, the park and estate by then having grown considerably due to purchases and by allotments under the Chapel Allerton Enclosure Act. Incidentally, the conveyance included '... all that pew, seat or sitting being number 44 in the middle aisle of the Episcopal Chapel of Chapel Allerton now or late in the occupation of Joseph Lees.'

Christopher Beckett (1777-1847), JP, a Deputy Lord Lieutenant of the West Riding and twice Mayor of Leeds, resided at Meanwood Park, as it came to be known, and was noted for his '... support of the calls of religion and the claims of charity.' He made alterations and additions to the south side of the Hall about 1830, the architect being John Clark, and extensively increased his Meanwood estate by other purchases. After his death in 1847 his unmarried sisters, Mary and Elizabeth, continued to live at the Hall until their deaths in 1858 and 1864 respectively.

Christopher, a bachelor, died without having made a will and the property passed to his elder brother, Sir John Beckett (1775-1847), who died a few weeks later. All the Chapel Allerton property, which included Meanwood Park, together with the hereditary title, then passed to the next surviving brother, Thomas Beckett (1779-1872) of Somerby Park, Gainsborough. His daughter, Mary, a spinster, inherited a life interest but it was to the children of his younger daughter, Elizabeth, wife of Sir Henry Hickman Bacon, that the estate finally passed.

After the death in 1864 of Christopher Beckett's sister, Elizabeth, Meanwood Park was once again occupied by tenants, the first being Christopher's nephew, William Beckett Denison. The Hall was unoccupied from about 1872 until 1875 when it was let to Joshua Bower who was joined in the following year by his brother, R. W. Bower, both described as colliery owners; it is a local tradition that the two brothers, who dined together, never spoke to one another. R. W. Bower appears to have been the last ordinary tenant of Meanwood Park.

The Hall was destined to have one more private and probably rent free occupier - John Ford Smart, the woodman, perhaps employed by the Beckett family. He lived in the woodman's cottage almost on the edge of the quarry, the worked out part of which was used in 1917 and 1918 for the testing of guns made in Hunslet. Because of the noise and damage to his cottage he made a strong plea for a house at a safe distance from the quarry and the Smart family of five was moved into the Hall, which it was said had enough rooms to provide ten for each member of the family!

In 1919 Leeds Corporation rented Meanwood Park to provide a 'colony' for the mentally handicapped, which was formally opened on 3 June 1920, although the first patient had been admitted in the previous year. In 1921 the Corporation bought the Meanwood Park estate and surrounding land totalling in all one hundred and seventy-eight acres, from Sir Hickman

Beckett Bacon of Thonock, Gainsborough, grandson of Sir Thomas Beckett. Originally eighty-seven patients were accommodated in the Hall, but during the following twenty years villas were built in the grounds and by 1941 beds were provided for eight hundred and forty-one patients. The Hall, by then referred to as 'The Mansion', was used for other hospital purposes. Meanwood Park Hospital was taken over by the National Health Service in 1948 and administered by Leeds (Group B) Hospital Management Committee. It is now the responsibility of the Leeds Eastern Health Authority and accommodates about four hundred and sixty residents.

Early in the nineteenth century there were a few small cottages close to Meanwood Hall which were owned by the Overseers of the Poor of Chapel Allerton. It appears that Robert Denison did not like these dwellings near to his mansion so they were demolished, the site being exchanged for a plot of land on the edge of the Park on which were built four single storey cottages for the poor. In July 1845 the record and account book of the Overseers states 'The committee agrees to Mr. Beckett's proposal respecting the removal of the poor houses, provided the committee approve the scite [sic] of the buildings proposed to be erected.' Later in the same year at a special meeting this matter was considered again when it was agreed '... that the scite adjoining the Alwoodley Road near John Glow's house be selected for the new poor houses, and that Mr. Oates and the Overseers be requested to inspect the scite and houses during their erection.' The four poor houses to be replaced were occupied in 1844 by Widow Stead, Hamer Higgins, Thomas Walker and Widow Midgley. Whether or not the new poor houses were ever built on the Alwoodley Road (King Lane) is not known but as Christopher Beckett died within two years of the scheme being approved it is possible that no action was taken.

The four single storey cottages 'for the poor', now demolished, which were on the edge of the Park (Parkside Road) were included in the property bought by the Corporation in 1921 and transferred to the Health Authority in 1948.

Even before Christopher Beckett bought Meanwood Hall, however, his younger brother, William (1784-1863), had purchased three closes of land and a parcel of wood ground at Woodside in 1810 together with a considerable tract of land to the east of Stonegate Road. William, a very rich banker, was a considerable force in the commercial affairs of Leeds which he represented in Parliament. For a time his residence was Kirkstall Grange (formerly New Grange) in Beckett's Park - now part of Leeds Polytechnic, formerly the City of Leeds Training College. After he died his Meanwood property came under the control of his younger brother, Edmund Beckett (1787-1874), who married Maria Beverley. This union linked the Denison and Beckett families as Maria was the heiress of Lady Ann Denison wife of Sir Thomas Denison (1697-1765) a kinsman of Thomas Denison, the builder of Meanwood Hall. Lady Ann's trustees purchased the Manor of

Grimthorpe in the East Riding which ultimately devolved on Maria, and Edmund assumed the name and arms of Denison. On his succession to the Baronetcy in 1872 when his brother Thomas died, however, he discontinued the name Denison and became Sir Edmund Beckett.

His eldest son, Edmund Beckett Denison (1816-1905), QC, MP, who also relinquished the name Denison, was created Baron Grimthorpe in 1886. Recognised as an authority on clocks, he invented a three-legged escapement, later used in all good turret clocks. Baron Grimthorpe and his wife, Fanny Catharine, daughter of the late Rt Rev. John Lonsdale, Bishop of Lichfield, are buried close to the north side of St Alban's Cathedral of which Lord Grimthorpe was a great benefactor.

The Meanwood property of this branch of the family was finally sold to Leeds Corporation and Ernest Haley in 1919 and 1939 respectively by Ralph William Ernest Beckett, Third Baron Grimthorpe.

24. **Sir John Beckett,** Second Baronet, brother of Christopher who purchased Meanwood Hall.

25. **Meanwoodside** — interior in the days of the Kitson Clarks.

Meanwoodside

It is over thirty years since the house known as Meanwoodside, which stood in Meanwood Park near the Green Road entrance, was demolished. It is to be regretted that so many members of the community have no recollection of that handsome, well proportioned building of fine ashlar with a deeply eaved roof of green slate, which was erected by Edward Oates in 1838-39.

This spot, however, had been a habitation site long before the nineteenth century. A branch of the Whalley family (widespread to the north of Leeds) was well established in the old Chapel Allerton township at least from the late sixteenth century. As already indicated the whole area was, from the thirteenth century, in the hands of the Abbot of Kirkstall and it is known that the Whalleys were paying rent to the Abbey at the time of the dissolution in 1539.

Thomas was a favourite baptismal name for the eldest Whalley son in each generation. There were six successive Thomas Whalleys at Meanwoodside otherwise Weetwoodside (as the area was then known) between about 1600 and 1750. On 12 May 1656 'Thomas Whalley the elder of Chapel Allerton, tanner...', made a will leaving'... my sonne, Thomas Whalley, the Tanhouse with the pits...'. The provisions of this will, while detailed, are most complicated but'... the low parlour in which I now dwell with chamber over...' (no doubt an old timber framed structure) must have been the forerunner of 'Whalley House' which appears in the picture alongside Edward Oates's new house. The 'Whalley House', which dated from the late seventeenth or early eighteenth century, indicates the growing prosperity of the family through their farming and tanning activities, and it was probably a grandson of the above Thomas - another Thomas - who could afford to rebuild in the 'new style'.

The increasing wealth of the Whalleys about this time is confirmed by the purchase by Thomas in 1690 of messuages or tenements and several closes bounded on the north by 'The Meanwood' and on the south by Headingley

26. **Meanwoodside** — as built by Edward Oates in 1838, with the old Whalley House.

Moor and the lands of Daniel Foxcroft. During the following decades further piecemeal acquisitions of land were negotiated.

The tannery mentioned, which stood at the foot of Hollin Lane between the beck and the goit, later became Holmes's Farm, which after a period of neglect and dereliction has lately been rebuilt as three attractive dwellings.

The last Meanwoodside Whalley, Francis, who died in 1784, left the residue of his Meanwood estate to his grand-niece, Ann Rinder, and after her death to her children. When a sale was contemplated in 1833, counsel pointed to a problem saying 'As long as Ann Rinder is alive despite her great age, the title is strictly not marketable, on account of the legal, tho' not real, possibility of more issue.' Ann Rinder was then aged 78!

The Rinders were absentee landlords for fifty years during which time they let the house and tannery, but grossly neglected the fabric. The 1833 sale notice described it as 'A genteel stone & slated messuage...', but a survey by Wm Wilson, a local builder, reported the buildings to be derelict and that 'The back of the House is not inhabited nor can it be; the ceiling and false roof is bent down and falling from the rain... the roof being open to the day...'. The front was little better and Wilson added 'We consider it very dangerous to dwell in.'

Nothwithstanding the state of the property and the legal problems, Edward Oates bought the estate and built his home on the site of the ramshackle farm buildings at the back of the old 'Whalley House'. He married Susan Grace, thus uniting two prominent cloth merchant families of Leeds. Edward died in 1865 and it was Susan who later demolished the old Whalley farm house and built on its foundations the extension to Meanwoodside.

Edward and Susan had three sons (two other children died in infancy). The eldest, Francis (Frank), a great explorer and Fellow of the Royal Geographical Society, died of fever in Bechuanaland in 1875. He is said to have been one of the first Europeans to have seen the Victoria Falls in full flood. The second son, William Edward, also a FRGS and explorer, who died in Funchal, Madeira, was the father of Lawrence Edward Grace Oates, the gallant Captain Oates of *Scott's Last Expedition*. Although Captain Oates was born in Putney and not at Meanwoodside, he was a frequent visitor in the time of his uncle, Charles George Oates, from whom he inherited the estate in equal shares with his brother, Bryan William Grace Oates (see the plaque at the bottom of Memorial Drive leading to the Parish Church). The third son, the last Oates to live here, was Charles George (1844-1902), a barrister-at-law and animal lover. He was a charitable but retiring man who, according to his obituary, '...did good by stealth.'

The last owner was Lt Col Edwin Kitson Clark, TD, FSA, a prominent Leeds citizen, who rented the property from 1904 to 1917 when he bought the estate. Dying in 1942 he left a life interest to his widow, Georgina, and when she died in 1954 Leeds Corporation purchased Meanwoodside.

The intention was to make the house into a natural history 'trailside' museum with a Polar room to commemorate Capt. Oates. Unfortunately the cost of putting the building into a proper state of repair was thought not to be justified and it was demolished soon after.

The once secluded and very private property is now a public place (part of Meanwood Park) but, although the house and formal gardens have gone, visitors to Meanwoodside will find evidence of the three families who lived there during three centuries - particularly in the landscaping by Edward Oates with its dams, waterfalls and numerous bridges over the watercourses and the unusual trees of which the tulip tree is a beautiful example.

At the end of Green Road adjoining the park stands Ivy Cottage. Facing south across the beck this attractive early nineteenth century gable fronted stone house was part of the purchase made by Edward Oates in 1834. Among the many occupants were John Elsworth, parish clerk and gardener from 1882, and later his son Alfred, a local artist with a studio in Briggate.

At this point it is appropriate also to mention Hollin House which stands on the other side of the beck and goit, near the Headingley entrance to Meanwoodside. Once known as Manklin's farm, and later as Snow's, the property dates at least from the mid-seventeenth century. The Oates family became the owners in 1796 and Edward, who inherited the farm in 1824 from his father, Joseph, late of Weetwood Hall, re-modelled the old house incorporating some of the former structure.

Carr Manor formerly **Carr House**

George Oates (1717-1779), merchant of Potternewton, second son of Joseph Oates of Chickenley and later of Leeds, bought Carr House with about fifty acres of land and a share of the manor and lordship of Chapel

27. **Carr Manor**

Allerton from Christopher Nevile of Emmanuel College, Cambridge in 1765. The property was the inheritance of Christopher's grandmother, Elizabeth Sharpe, daughter of Edith Saxton a descendant of Thomas Marshall who, with three other local yeomen, purchased the manor and lordship of Chapel Allerton from the Crown in 1602.

When George Oates died, Carr House passed to his son, Joseph, of Weetwood Hall and thence to his eldest son, George, who died in 1832 when the estate went to his younger brother, Joseph Henry.

Fifteen years after Joseph Henry's death in 1868, Carr House with twenty-one acres was sold to Thomas Clifford Allbutt, MD. He built a new house designed by E. S. Prior, which is described by Derek Linstrum in *Historic Architecture of Leeds* as being '... in the Yorkshire manor-house tradition ...'. This house was built in 1881, as indicated by the date on the large iron gates, although the sale was not completed until 1883 when the property, at that time re-named Carr Manor, was described in the conveyance as '... recently erected by Thomas Clifford Allbutt.' The old stable block bearing the date 1796 was retained. Dr Allbutt was the eminent physician practising in Leeds who invented the pocket or short clinical thermometer. Leaving Meanwood in 1889 to take up an appointment as a Commissioner in Lunacy, he was later knighted and became Regius Professor of Physic at Cambridge University.

The next owner was Col Frederick William Tannett-Walker, an engineer. The Tannett-Walkers sold the estate in 1914 to the then Sir Berkeley George Andrew Moynihan, son of Captain Andrew Moynihan, VC. Sir Berkeley, a Leeds surgeon of distinction, became Lord Moynihan in 1929. He died in 1936 and two years later Carr Manor was purchased by Leeds Corporation as lodgings for High Court Judges when sitting in Leeds.

Housing

John Tuke's map of 1781 shows very few buildings in the area now known as Meanwood. Meanwood Hall, Meanwoodside, and Carr Manor, already described, are shown together with a thin scatter of smaller buildings particularly in the vicinity of Parkside Road, Stonegate Road and Green Road. There were also small clusters of buildings along the beck, and two isolated farms, namely Bywater Farm (near Scotland Mill) and the other near King Alfred's Castle. The story would, however, be incomplete without a few details of the earlier cottages, the medium sized dwellings, and the housing developments of the period 1800-1939.

The name Meanwood was printed on old maps in what is now the Parkside Road area, whereas the Green Road locality was known as Meanwoodside or Woodside. Incidentally Meanwood Road was the name given to Parkside Road on the 1812 Enclosure Award map and it seems therefore, that this was where the original Meanwood village was to be found. Understandably the earliest inhabitants would choose the spring-line on the higher better drained land for their buildings rather than the valley bottom. It was a ribbon development between the ancient Stonegate Road near Alder Hill Cottages and the house formerly on the site of Fairfax, both strongly built seventeenth century buildings. The meaner dwellings of that period, in all probability single storey cottages, have perished as have some of their successors of the nineteenth century such as Shires's farmhouse (which stood almost opposite Fairfax), Myrtle Square and many others near The Bay Horse. Nos. 58, 60 and 62, Parkside Road dating from the mid eighteenth century, however, have survived.

* * * * *

Brief details of Fairfax, Alder Hill Cottages, and Myrtle Square are as follows:

Fairfax

The property bought by Matthew Sawer in 1801, on part of which he built his tannery, included a number of dwellings one of which stood where Fairfax is today.

Edmund Bogg in his book *The Old Kingdom of Elmet* published in 1904, says of that building 'To a decrepit house, standing with its gable end to the old Pack Horse Road at Hill Top, local tradition ascribes the distinction of being the oldest in Meanwood. ... It was the first hostel in this district. Over the door the words "Tap, W. P." ... and the date 1630, may still be deciphered, flanked by the convential bush ... which, in the 17th century, took the place of the living bough hung out as the sign of a place of entertainment for man and beast.'

Decrepit was an apt description for when the property was sold in 1905 by Jane Sawer and trustees to Thomas Wright and James Annandale Town, leather manufacturers, it was described as 'Disused buildings, formerly three cottages, in the occupation of Ann Walsh.'

Shortly after 1905 most of the buildings were demolished and the house re-erected at a right angle to the previous one using the stonework, including the kneelers and pinnacles, of the old buildings. It must be assumed that this work was done by Wright and Town, who in 1911 sold the premises (then known as Hawcaster House) to their firm Thomas Wright & Co. Ltd, Meanwood Road, from which it was bought by Dr H. Willcox in 1947.

If Edmund Bogg is correct in his belief that the original building was a place of entertainment this must have been the first public house in Meanwood.

Town had purchased the adjacent Meanwood Grove in 1904 from the Sawers; Alice, widow of Thomas Bradley, owned this property in 1775 and it became part of Matthew Sawer's estate in 1812.

Alder Hill Cottages

No. 1 Alder Hill Cottages, Stonegate Road, with the date A.D. 1635 over the door must be the oldest house in Meanwood to remain more or less as it was built. In all probability it was part of the estate of the Marshall family who owned the site of Carr House (Carr Manor) and other Meanwood property in the seventeenth and eighteenth centuries.

The earliest documentary evidence identifying the property is a deed of 1750 when the executors of Thomas Bombey sold to John Banks sixteen acres of land and buildings. A few years later Banks purchased a further three acres from Marmaduke Prince, land described as bounded on the east by the Stand Beck (Stainbeck) and on the south and west by the property previously bought by Banks. A further deed of 1779 records that the property was in the occupation of Sally Banks, spinster of Woodside, Chapel Allerton, who was allotted a further five acres by the Chapel Allerton Enclosure Award.

William Whitehead, farmer, was the owner occupier in 1844 by which time a barn adjacent to his house had been converted into three cottages. Twenty years later Theophilia Whitehead, widow, was a life tenant and in 1875 the property was bought by Benjamin Rowley, sand merchant of Headingley. At that time the occupiers were Eliza Marshall (one of the vendors), William Fall, Malachial Whittaker, James Barritt, George Williams and William Oddy.

These cottages were sold by the Rowley family in 1926.

29. **Alder Hill Cottages**

31. **Providence Square**

28. **Ancient House, Parkside Road**, rebuilt as Fairfax.

30. **Green Row**

Myrtle Square

The largest cottage development in Meanwood during the last century was Myrtle Square off Parkside Road built by Samuel Mitchell. He was the owner in 1825 of about one acre of land known as Lane End Field, Meanwood Lane (Parkside Road) and had by 1844 erected a small detached cottage on the roadside and a building facing east known as The Myrtle Tavern adjoining which and facing south were five cottages. Among these cottages there were two stables one of which became a joiner's shop and the other a store for the inn. Over the store and entered by steps between the former stables was a Roman Catholic meeting room which closed when St Urban's Church was built in Brookfield Road in 1902.

Shortly after 1844 a butcher's shop was erected between the detached cottage and the inn; the cottage became a brewhouse which with the former butcher's shop is now part of the Myrtle premises. At the same time the square was completed by the building of fourteen cottages facing east (one slightly larger than the others being occupied by the Mitchell family), six in the south-east corner and one more near the tavern. The latter was used for a few years as a Wesleyan Methodist Mission room. Part of a further building, also near the tavern, was made into a slaughter-house.

A plan of the site in 1914 shows that in the square there were pig stys, coal houses, a wash house, a greenhouse and three blocks of WCs, two of which were described as 'three lever' and 'eight lever' respectively.

The cottages, tavern and outbuildings, were sold by the trustees of Samuel Mitchell to John Smith's Tadcaster Brewery Co. Ltd in 1914 and by 1959 all the buildings except the inn had been demolished.

*   *   *   *   *

Early in the nineteenth century the centre of activity moved down the hill towards the beck and a few rows of dwellings were erected in the Green Road locality for the artisans and labourers employed nearby. These new terraces included:

Green Row and Providence Square

Where Green Chase and Church Close are today there were in 1768 eight cottages owned by Ann Sowden, widow, and her two daughters, Faith, wife of William Waite, and Sarah, wife of John Kent, but by 1804 the number had been reduced to four. Soon after eight new cottages called Green Row had been built by Thomas Waite and when he died he owned twelve cottages in the row and eight in Providence Square. In 1844 the Green Row property was sold by William Waite to Daniel Atkinson whose widow and son sold nine of the cottages to Samuel Smith of the Meanwood Tannery in 1870. The back walls of some of the Providence Square cottages and others that were in Church Lane still remain, separating this new property from a few of the gardens in Holmwood Avenue.

Tannery Square and Bywater Buildings

In 1815 Thomas Bumby mortgaged to John Morris of Woodside, a local tanner, two cottages with an orchard and garden described as in Low Woodside, and in 1822 Morris bought the property. Fifteen years later he had built eight cottages on the site, the two original cottages having been demolished. The tenants were William Senior, Samuel Renton, John Webster, John Wilkinson, William Sandiforth, Mary Lindley, Samuel Goodall and John Beckwith.

32. **Tannery Square** and **Bywater Buildings**

These cottages were called Tanners Row by the time Matthew Bywater bought them in 1846 from the son of John Morris, deceased, and his widow, Mary. Six years later Bywater bought land on the west side of the row from Sir Thomas Beckett on which he subsequently built six houses known as Bywater Buildings and in 1872 his son, Matthew, sold all this property to Emma Jane Arden of Headingley.

Bywater Buildings were back-to-back houses, those facing east together with Tanners Row became Tannery Square and those facing west retained the name Bywater Buildings.

Most of this property was purchased by Leeds Corporation about 1967 and, with the exception of two cottages now one dwelling house in private ownership, was renovated and made into flats financed by the British Council and the Mary Morris Student Housing Association, for married students from overseas at Leeds University.

Brick Row

James Martin, the paper-maker of Wood Mills, bought a plot of land in 1810, formerly part of Chapel Allerton Common, from John Midgley and it was on this land that the first Methodist Chapel was built in 1811.

By his will made in 1847 Martin left to his three daughters, Ann, Averilda and Elizabeth, '... eight recently erected brick cottages with the piece of ground in front.' which he had built on the land purchased previously. It is not known if the villagers were concerned that these cottages were not built of stone but this cannot have been popular with the local quarrymen and stonemasons.

By this time brick was in common use in Leeds for house building but it was to be about another forty years before any more houses constructed entirely of brick were built in Meanwood. There were, however, at least two small blocks built about 1870 which had brick west end walls, perhaps a compromise between cost and the demands of local industry.

Brick Row, now demolished, was near the former Chapel - presently occupied by builders' merchants.

Hustler's Row

Of all the Meanwood cottage developments of the last century the most unusual was Hustler's Row. Edward Oates wrote in his diary in May 1850 'The twenty cottages of Mr. Husler now completed in the most extraordinary situation.'

33. **Hustler's Row**

Two years previously John Husler, quarry owner, leased from Henry Charles Englefield for twenty-one years the land on which he built these cottages, the ground rent being £15 0s. 0d. per annum, very probably the only development in Meanwood on land not owned by the builder. It must be assumed that with his access to stone and the housing needs of his employees, Husler considered this would be a worthwhile venture notwithstanding that at the end of the lease the cottages would become the property of the landowner.

When the Englefield estate was put up for sale in 1858 Oates bought Hustler's Row together with other property adjoining his estate. In 1871 there were one hundred and six occupants in these twenty cottages and the two others, now demolished, which were at the far end of the row.

*   *   *   *   *

Many professional men and businessmen migrated from the centre of Leeds to Headingley and Chapel Allerton in the nineteenth century and a few built their residences in Meanwood of which the following are examples:

Meanwood Towers

The house in Meanwood which frequently prompts questions is Meanwood Towers, particularly by people who remember the very conspicuous and unusual chimneys which were shortened in 1969 as they were unsafe. A comment often made is 'Did the chimneys really resemble organ pipes?' - not an unreasonable question having regard to the history of the building.

In 1866 Thomas Stuart Kennedy, machine maker, commissioned Edward W. Pugin, son of the celebrated architect, Augustus W. N. Pugin, to design a house for him. In the same year he commenced negotiations with Schulze & Sons of Paulinzelle, Germany, to build an organ for his wife in their new home. The house was built in 1867, although the sale by Joshua Buckton, Alexander Crawford and Mary Oates to Kennedy of thirty-four acres of land on the west side of Stonegate Road with the right to draw water from the Revolution Well, was not completed until 13 June 1868!

Negotiations were still in progress regarding the proposed organ and it was finally decided to build a detached centrally heated wooden organ house in the grounds of the building, once known as Meanwood House. The organ house, capable of seating eight hundred people, was completed in May 1869 and later that year Edmund Schulze came to Meanwood and stayed with the Kennedys for some months to 'voice' the instrument in the building. When completed it was formally 'opened' by Samuel Sebastian Wesley, one time organist at Leeds Parish Church, grandson of the famous hymn writer Charles Wesley and great-nephew of John Wesley, founder of Methodism. Wesley was only persuaded to give the opening recital on condition that no one would be present except Mr & Mrs Kennedy, Edmund Schulze and

Thomas C. Allbutt, a very good friend of Kennedy who had been closely associated with the purchase of the organ.

34. **Meanwood Towers** with original ornamental chimneys.

Unfortunately due to ill health Mrs Kennedy was advised to discontinue playing the organ and as there were problems in controlling the heating of the building and in its maintenance owing to dampness, Kennedy decided to sell the instrument. It was bought by the Misses Carter of Harrogate and installed in St Peter's Church, Harrogate, in 1877 but following disagreement they sold the organ to Henry William Eyres who presented it to St Bartholomew's Church, Armley, in 1879 where it still provides inspiration and enjoyment. The brief details about the organ have been extracted from a booklet *The Armley Schulze Organ* by Kenneth I. Johnstone published in 1985 (second edition) - a very comprehensive and fascinating account of this world famous organ.

Kennedy sold the house in 1886 to William D. Cliff of Armley who lived there until 1916.

Meanwood Towers is described by Derek Linstrum as '... using gables, ornamental chimney stacks and oriel windows in abandoned profusion.' It is now converted into flats and although the marble staircase remains much of the oak panelling has gone, the organ house having long since disappeared.

Alder Hill

Benjamin Rowley, who owned Alder Hill Cottages and adjacent land, in 1879 sold to his son, Walter, a mining engineer, two acres of the estate, the deed referring to a dwellinghouse in course of erection - the present Alder

Hill, now converted into flats. It is not known when the lodge in Stonegate Road was built but the date on one of the gate posts is Anno Domini 1887 and on the other are the initials RWM - for Rowley, Walter and Mary his wife. On the gates which no longer exist were the welcoming words 'THROUGH THIS WIDE AND OPEN GATE NONE COME TOO EARLY NONE TOO LATE' and over the door of the house is inscribed 'WELCOME THE COMING SPEED THE GOING GUEST'. Alder Hill was sold by the executors of Walter Rowley, late Major, Royal Engineers in 1926.

A number of the more substantial dwellings have been demolished over the years for development of the sites. They include Bentley House on the west side of Bentley Lane, Bentley Lodge which stood on the site of the present Meanwood Health Centre, Meanwood Lodge at the corner of Green Road and Stonegate Road, and Daisy Bank at the junction of Green Road and Church Lane.

* * * * *

Towards the end of the last century numerous terraces of brick built houses were erected including Greenwood Mount, Bentley Lane and those between there and Monk Bridge Road. The Highburys were also built at this time, and although in Headingley they were closely related to Meanwood as many of the occupants were employed at Highbury Works. All this coincided with the establishment of a good public transport service which ended the old pattern of Meanwood residents in general working locally.

The housing scheme which changed the life of the village more than any other, however, was the building of the Meanwood estate shortly after the first World War. These houses, built by the Corporation under the 1919 Housing Act, were described as 'homes fit for heroes to live in' and, having amenities far better than many of the other working class houses in the area, they were very much in demand. Most of the one hundred and seventy-nine acres on which the Stonegates, Stainbecks and Farm Hills were built, had been bought by William Beckett in 1810 and had been in the ownership of the Beckett family since that time. There were only three houses on this land when it was bought by the Corporation - Kent House, Stainbeck Avenue; Hodgson's Farm, Stonegate Road (now demolished), with eighty-six acres; and Model Farm, Farm Hill, with eighty acres.

Inevitably there was local concern about this extensive new development on farm land and at the loss of its ground by at least one cricket club; also the style of building of these 'white houses' of concrete slabs was not received with favour in the village.

Within three years eight hundred houses had been built, most of them with three bedrooms but a few with four, their large gardens being a much publicised feature of the estate. The roads had grass verges but many years later they were tar-macadammed and painted green! In 1985 it was decided

35. **Meanwood Housing Estate**

that, due to structural deterioration, all these houses would have to be demolished. Initially they were allocated from a waiting list made up of overseas ex-servicemen who came from all parts of Leeds, and with the many new and mainly young families coming to Meanwood it was not long before there was an acute shortage of school places. This was met by the completion of the infants' department at Bentley Lane School in 1925 and the mixed senior school in 1929.

The late 1920s and 1930s was the era of house building for private ownership, the principal developments being the Parklands, Parksides, Sunsets, Church Avenue and on the south side of Green Road.

The last housing scheme on farm land (Church Farm) was the Holmwood Estate, built in 1964-65, and numerous old stone dwellings in and around the Green Road area have been replaced in recent years by houses and flats.

Inns, Taverns and Public Houses

In spite of considerable research it is not possible to say which of Meanwood's public houses is the oldest. However, it is known that earlier than the Myrtle, Bay Horse or first Beckett's Arms there were at least three other public houses or beer-houses in the village.

One, The Star, is mentioned in a deed of 1810 but the building had even then ceased to be used as a public house. It was in the area of Stonegate Road, and very probably in the older buildings of what was latterly known as Hodgson's Farm, now demolished, where Stonegate Farm Close is today. Another, also in Stonegate Road, was the present stone house facing down the hill on the west side of the road near Parkside Avenue. According to the Chapel Allerton survey of 1804 this public house, owned by John Rinder, was occupied by Robert Harrison. The other was on the north side of the 'S' bend in Parkside Road (alias Dunbar Hill/Dunny Hill/Tannery Hill) which in local directories from 1814 to 1839 is named The Woodcock, occupied by Benjamin Marshall, and from 1849 to 1853 by Martha Marshall. The Tithe Award of 1844 gives the owner as Christopher Beckett and the occupier as Benjamin Marshall. When Christopher purchased Meanwood Hall in 1824 there was a reference in the conveyance, however, to a public house on the estate called The Woodpecker once occupied by William Clarkson and later by William Marshall. This was the same establishment as The Woodcock tenanted in 1814 by Benjamin Marshall, very probably the son and under-tenant of William.

The situation of this tavern may seem to be a very out of the way spot for a public house in those days but being on the road described in 1763 as the King's Highway from Chapel Allerton to Horsforth, it would have been a very welcome stopping place for the traveller. It was also easily accessible to the men working in the local tanneries, quarries, mills and on the farms in the area.

By 1861 the Woodcock or Woodpecker had become the Well House Inn, in the tenancy of George Dunbar. After his death, his widow, Hannah, because of the smallness of the building changed it to 'off licence'. According to both local and family tradition this change had little effect on sales because all the 'regulars' borrowed pint pots from nearby cottages and, winter and summer alike, drank their ale in a corner of the field behind the building and boasted that their tap-room had the highest ceiling of any in the country! This little beer-house ceased to exist when Hannah Dunbar moved up the hill and took over the Bay Horse in 1884, and the building was demolished about fifty years ago.

The following details of the existing public houses have been obtained from various sources including the title deeds of the properties and Leeds directories.

The Myrtle Tavern

One, Henry Cooper, sold about an acre of land known as Lane End Field in 1820 to Thomas Midgley, who the next day borrowed £500 from Benjamin Clarkson and assigned the land to him for a thousand years. With the agreement of Clarkson, the field was sold in 1824 to Joseph Horsman and James Gray and, with the consent of all concerned, Horsman's half share was transferred to Samuel Mitchell. Next year Mitchell bought Gray's half share and by 1834 he had erected buildings on the land, one of which was The Myrtle Tavern occupied by John Mitchell, ale and porter dealer. James Oddy, butcher and innkeeper, of a well known local family, was the tenant in 1861.

The Myrtle tavern and adjoining property, remained in the ownership of Samuel Mitchell until his death in 1872; his will stipulated that his land and buildings should not be sold until after the death of the last survivor of his children: John, James, Jane Ann Oddy, George, and Mary Lindley Whitehead.

Samuel Oddy leased the tavern in 1911 on a year to year basis at a rent of £50 per annum, subject to his using his best endeavours to increase and extend the custom of the business and to his living on the premises.

On 7 September 1914, following the death of Mary L. Whitehead earlier that year, the trustees of Samuel Mitchell, one of whom was Dr F. A. Lees, sold the property to John Smith's Tadcaster Brewery Co. Ltd who extended the premises in 1974.

36. **The Myrtle Tavern**

37. **The Myrtle** and corner of **Myrtle Square** with well remembered pear tree.

The Bay Horse

James Prince, a stonemason, was allotted two roods and fourteen perches of land under the Chapel Allerton Enclosure Act of 1813 on what is the present Parkside Road. He sold this land, a small quarry, to Joseph Horsman on which by 1826 Joseph had built several cottages. Two years later Horsman borrowed £460 from Joshua Wood, the agreement stating that he had begun to erect other cottages.

James England, ale and porter dealer, was occupier of the Grey Horse at Meanwood in 1837 and the 1844 Tithe Award confirms his tenancy under Joseph Horsman and that the Grey Horse was on the site of the present Bay Horse.

Horsman died in 1855 when the property passed to his three unmarried daughters, Ann, Ellen and Jane, who in 1876 repaid the heiress of Joshua Wood the money borrowed by their father. Next day they mortgaged the inn, by then known as The Bay Horse, and the cottages for £460 to four Wesleyan Methodist ministers: Revs. S. J. Bush of Edinburgh, J. Reacher of Croydon, R. Newton Young of London and S. Cooke of Walsingham. The occupier of the inn at that time was Sarah Farrar, widow of William Farrar who had been the tenant in 1861, and Sarah was succeeded by George Wilson.

In 1884, Ann, the last survivor of the Horsman sisters, and the four

74

Wesleyan ministers, sold The Bay Horse and the cottages to Hannah Dunbar who died in 1892. The inn was then taken over by her son, Isaac Alfred Dunbar, who that year leased the property to John Smith's Tadcaster Brewery Co. Ltd for fourteen years. Dunbar, and persons to whom he had previously mortgaged The Bay Horse, sold it in 1922 (at that time the headquarters of the Meanwood Bowling Club) with the adjacent cottages to John Smith's who extended the premises at the back in about 1927.

The front part of the inn was originally three cottages but it is very probable that only one of them was the 1837 inn.

38.　**The Bay Horse**

The Beckett's Arms - formerly the Dusty Miller

The first Beckett's Arms, which had the appearance of two adjoining old cottages with a later building, stood right up to the junction of Meanwood Road and Monk Bridge Road, with an entrance in Meanwood Road and a side entrance up a short flight of stone steps in Monk Bridge Road.

The early history of this spot is obscure, but in 1810 John Laidman (or Lademan), sold to John Rollinson of Headingley, land and buildings at Meanwoodside which with additional cottages erected by him, he then sold to William Scott of Headingley in 1826.

In 1834 an inn on this site known as the Dusty Miller was occupied by George Askey but by 1839 the tenant was Susannah Askey the name of the inn by then having changed to The Beckett's Arms. The landlord in 1847 was James Burley and eleven years later there was a settlement in contemplation

39. **The Beckett's Arms**

40. **The old Beckett's Arms** with part of the present inn on the left.

41. **The Meanwood**

of marriage between Hannah Burley, widow and innkeeper of The Beckett's Arms, and James Naylor, stonemason of Meanwoodside. Attached to the settlement is an inventory listing the public rooms of the inn as tap-room, bar-room and lodge-room, and among the contents were thirty spittoons!

William Scott died in 1848 and in 1869 his grandson, also William Scott, sold to James Naylor, innkeeper, property described as 'All that triangular plot of land situate at Meanwoodside ... and also all the dwellinghouse and other buildings erected thereon ... in the several occupations of James Naylor, who occupied part of the dwellinghouse and buildings as an inn or public house known by the sign of The Beckett's Arms, and of Joseph Johnson and John Martin.'

Naylor died in 1872 and was succeeded by his son, Josiah, who with Hannah Naylor, widow, and others sold the property to Robert Cross in 1877. After extending the premises on the Meanwood Road frontage, Cross and mortgagees including Henry Herbert Riley-Smith and Frank Riley-Smith, sold the property to John Smith's Tadcaster Brewery Co. Ltd in 1896. The conveyance records that one, Alfred Brown, had originally agreed to purchase the property but that he had subsequently contracted to sell it to John Smith's for £1,100 more than the purchase price he had negotiated with Cross!

The present Beckett's Arms was built in 1939 around the old inn which was then demolished.

The Meanwood

In 1925 a small plot of land which had been owned by the Beckett family since 1810 was sold by the Third Baron Grimthorpe to The Leeds and Wakefield Breweries Ltd. The Meanwood, built on this land, was licensed and opened on 26 July 1927, the licence having been transferred from The Smithfield Hotel, North Street, which had lapsed in 1925. The establishment was later taken over by Melbourne Brewery Co. Ltd and then by Joshua Tetley and Son Ltd, the present owners.

This, the latest public house but with the very old name 'The Meanwood', must have been built as a direct result of the large increase in the number of local residents when the very extensive Meanwood housing estate was developed in the early 1920s.

The Lees Family

This section does not fit conveniently into any of the foregoing topics; it is necessary, therefore, to deal separately with the story of the three generations of this talented but wellnigh forgotten family that lived in the village for a period of more than one hundred years from early in the nineteenth century.

Joseph Lees was nineteen years old when he left his home at Stainland, Nr Halifax, to take up the post of usher at Ephraim Sanderson's school, St John's House, Aberford. He married Ephraim's youngest daughter, Anne, in 1814 and shortly after became the tenant of Meanwood Hall, with the intention of establishing a school, which was later described as '... an academy for young gentlemen.'

Located in what was then a remote situation the school must have been residential although no records have survived of the pupils who were educated there. The venture obviously prospered as Joseph had to add a new wing to the north of the Hall as a schoolroom; it is said that there were between eighty and one hundred scholars by 1815.

Unfortunately Anne died in that year, when only nineteen, two months after the birth of her son, Frederic Richard, who was looked after by his paternal grandmother then living at the Hall.

When Christopher Beckett bought Meanwood Hall in 1824, Joseph (who had remarried in 1816) had to leave. He originally intended to live in Hill Top House (now Fosse House) which he built for that purpose, but the family went instead to a farm in Cookridge, moving later to Headingley. In 1844 Joseph embarked upon a voyage of discovery to the West Coast of Africa!

Frederic Richard Lees (1815-1897) was sent to school in Bury, Lancashire, in 1825, and although he was later articled to a Leeds solicitor he did not complete his legal training but devoted his life to the cause of temperance. He was a prolific writer on the subject and addressed meetings and gave lectures throughout the country. An Honorary Doctorate of Philosophy was conferred on him in 1842 by the University of Giessen, Germany.

In 1853 he went to live at Meanwood Lodge, bought for him out of public subscriptions, where he received many notable visitors. The house stood at the junction of Green Road and Stonegate Road being described as 'An old fashioned uncomfortable house with front windows looking over sloping upland towards Headingley.'

He later lived in Watford but died at Halifax in May 1897 where he was staying prior to addressing a Band of Hope conference. Dr Lees was held in such high regard that the numbers attending the service at Meanwood churchyard conducted by the Vicar of Leeds far exceeded those expected. The Vicar of Meanwood was away at the time and an eleventh hour request that the Rev. Charles Garrett, a former President of the Wesleyan Methodist Conference and a temperance advocate, be allowed to make a grave side address was refused as this required the incumbent's approval. With the agreement of the family, however, an unscheduled service addressed by the Rev. Garrett and the Rev. W. L. Carter, a Congregational Minister, was held in the Wesleyan Chapel where mourners had met; this delayed the interment and led to a disturbance in the churchyard. The whole affair attracted national publicity and the *Leeds Mercury* reporting the funeral referred to it as a regrettable incident. In a subsequent letter to the paper Dr F. A. Lees expressed the family's regret at the controversy.

Frederic Arnold Lees (1847-1921), son of F. R. Lees, who spent his earlier years in the family home, Meanwood Lodge, and later lived in Bentley Lane, qualified as a doctor of medicine in 1871 and became a general practitioner.

He was, however, far more widely known as a botanist of distinction. He travelled extensively and wrote many articles and books about wild plants including one published in 1888 entitled *The Flora of West Yorkshire*. He was interested in the plants of the Meanwood Valley, especially those alien to this country found near the local fellmongeries, their fruits and seeds having been brought in the fleeces of sheep from various parts of the world.

His collection of wild plants comprising some twenty-five thousand specimens, which he sold to Bradford Corporation in 1906, may be seen by appointment at the Cartwright Hall, Bradford. A further collection he made is in the British Museum (Natural History Division), South Kensington.

Conclusion - Fact or Fiction

Although Meanwood is not an ancient village with its own medieval church and traditions going back to the distant past, it has acquired its own folk-lore. Some of the following tales are true but some may be apochryphal. They should stir the memory of the older reader; for newer members of the village they will provide a glimpse of a way of life which has gone for ever.

*   *   *   *   *

It is perhaps a hundred years or so since the old West Riding custom of 'Riding the Stang' was carried out at Meanwood. In cases of marital quarrels leading to wife beating, the culprit (or his effigy) was subjected to the ignominious punishment of being tied to a stang (a pole or beam) and carried, shoulder high, round the village accompanied by a jeering mob drumming on old cans and pans.

The daughter of the village constable at the turn of the century, used to tell of the Meanwood man whose wife was a drunkard. Her selling of all his furniture proved to be the last straw and he slit her throat Apprehended in his allotment trying to cut his own throat, he was tried for murder. The then Vicar of St Chad's Church became active in his defence which was based on extreme provocation; he was found guilty but sentenced to only ten years imprisonment. After serving his term he returned to live in the village, striking terror in the hearts of many: he was in reality a mild little man who in due course was again accepted by the inhabitants.

There may have been drunkenness and violence in the past but only one instance of riotous assembly in Meanwood has come to light - that was when the community felt it was being robbed of its time honoured rights. There is no written report of the incident but as late as 1935 it was related that within living memory the villagers led by the butcher had assembled, armed with pick-axes, and made a breach in a wall which had been built to 'stop' a road. The actual spot is not known but, at the time of the Enclosure of 1813, there was a 'Public Bridle Path and Private Carriage Road' which passed the back wall of Ivy Cottage, Green Road, (the cobbles are still there). This road led to Hollin Lane crossing the bridge which bears the inscription E.O. MDCCCXXXIV. The route had disappeared by 1892 and, as Charles George Oates is known to have won a court case concerning his estate, it seems fair to assume that it was the closing of this road through Meanwoodside which sparked off the trouble.

Why was the area between Green Road and Hustler's Row called 'Low Harrogate' during the last century? The local explanation was that it derived from the town Harrogate on account of the very pure air and water in the locality. It has been suggested, however, that it was a folk memory going back to the Dark Ages - a corruption of here + gata (army + road) - the way of the army - (Roman soldiers from Adel?). Failing early documentary evidence the suggestion must be dismissed as a fanciful romanticism.

The Whalley stone has been mentioned, but who was Kate Scholes? Her name with the date 1884 is carved on a boulder in a field near the path leading from Dunny Hill to Tongue Lane; and what about poor Hancock, whose memorial in the wall beside a path beyond Hustler's Row is a rock marked HANCOCK+ with the word shot on an adjacent stone? It was at this spot that Henry Trevor Wheeler Handcock, a Londoner aged twenty-six, shot himself on 11 September 1892. His body, which was taken to The Myrtle Tavern bottle store, was buried in Meanwood churchyard. Had he fallen out with the young lady in Leeds whom he was reported to have visited?

Near Cross Bentley Lane was a small quarry worked by a man named Fitzgerald, where early this century ganister rock was crushed by a metal edge-roller on a shaft turned by a horse (a horse-gin). During the first World War and at the time of the 1921 strike, soft coal was extracted from a thin seam between the bands of ganister and sold by the bucket to local people.

Mrs Kitson Clark of Meanwoodside gathered a fund of stories of old Meanwood at meetings of the Women's Institute: of the tailor/schoolmaster who used to sit cross-legged on a table while he sewed, with his pupils sitting around - probably in one of the cottages near the Meanwood Institute: of the horse bus plying to Leeds from the stables at Far Headingley (Hollin Lane): and of the tradition that top-boots were made in the village for really 'swanky' people who came down from London to have them measured and fitted individually. Based on its long history as a tanning centre, Meanwood may well have acquired a reputation for high class bespoke footwear. Certainly the census returns for the middle 1800s reveal a surprisingly large number of cordwainers/boot and shoe makers for such a small community.

Associated with Fairfax (already described) at the top of Dunny Hill is a tale known by very few. Referred to as 'The Irish Houses' by one or two of the former inhabitants of Hill Top, it was the centre of a little enclave of Irish people in the 1880s. One of the rebels suspected of the murder of Lord Frederick Cavendish, in Phoenix Park, Dublin, in 1882, sought refuge here among his kin, so the story goes. The police who searched the cottages failed to find him - he was clinging to the underneath of a bed frame, hidden by the ragged blankets and sacking draped on the bed. The police are supposed to have picked him up later. On a more mundane note, it might be added, the premises were used by Albert Illingworth in 1935 as 'The Summit Coal Depot' - his speciality being 'Summit small nuts' @ 1s. 3d. per cwt.!

A little further on, down Dunny Hill, on the right side of the road opposite Meanwood Grove, is an ever flowing spring stated in a deed of 1763 to be the 'Cold Bath commonly called Hazelwell' but in more recent times occasionally referred to locally as 'The Roman Well'. This was the site of the demolished Well House Inn, behind which stood a little bath-house. The *Leeds Intelligencer* of 18 July 1769, advertised 'This is to acquaint the Public, that the well known Cold Bath at Weetwood in the Parish of Leeds is now completely fitted up; where Ladies and Gentlemen may depend on civil usage by their most obedient humble Servant, Mary Wilson.' It was still used early in the present century but all that now remains is a depression in the ground with low stone walls on two sides.

At the turn of the century the Meanwood Mummers, led by John William Holliday, performed a version of the traditional St George play in the larger houses of the village at Christmas; the Church magazine for January 1885, in reporting the Christmas tea, commented '... our Handbell ringers provided some admirable music ...'. Of such was the simple entertainment of that time.

If 'The Battle of Meanwood' were not mentioned, many would consider the omission a mistake. They would point to the evidence of the 'Stainbeck' - the legend being that the stream ran red with blood - and to the musket balls, so many of which have been picked out of the beck at the foot of Woodhouse Ridge - or Pikeman Ridge, the suggestive name by which it was known in 1781. There may have been a Civil War skirmish hereabouts on 23 January 1643, but it can hardly have been a 'battle' - there is no documentary record of the incident. As for the circumstantial evidence, the name 'Staynbek' (i.e. Stonebeck) first appears in 1240, some four hundred years too soon, and Pikeman Ridge, or a very similar name, was used in 1561 - a hundred years before the date in question. As for the musket balls - their localised concentration suggests target practice rather than the spread of shot to be expected after an armed encounter.

The dams in the valley have claimed more than one life. There was the instance of a poor, distraught woman, intent on suicide, who asked some young children playing beside the Woodland Dye Works dam 'Which end is the deepest?' On a more cheerful note is an entry in the 1880 diary of Henry Harland, son of the village constable, recording the presentation of The Royal Humane Society's medal to J. F. Watmoor, a scholar of the Wesleyan Sunday School, for rescuing a small boy named Hartley from the Highbury dam. Six years later Alfred Perry, aged eight, was playing on the ice at Grey's dam, Weetwood, when it broke. A companion shouted for help and after considerable difficulty the boy was rescued by three young men namely: Kirk, Bumby and Tattersfield.

The mill dams were used for pleasure purposes. The big pond at Grove Mill, now the site of the large building of the Yorkshire Switchgear, was used privately by Alderman Boothroyd's family and friends for boating and no doubt for skating. In February 1929 - the year of the long hard frost - George Harland, manager at Highbury Works, had electric lights strung up round the dam, which became a popular rendezvous for skaters at 3d. per night.

Fosse House, Parkside Road, formerly known as Hill Top House and later as Meanwood Hill, was purchased by John Wilkinson of Carlton near Otley in 1830. It is of some interest as it was the early home of his daughter, Eliza, of whom few will have heard. After her father's death the family moved to Chapel Allerton and Eliza, orphaned when only fifteen years of age, kept the home together, caring for her brothers and sisters. She had often remarked that there were benevolent institutions for all sorts and conditions of people except unmarried women '... who are the most helpless of all.' On the day she died (of tuberculosis, which it is said, she caught from a dying man to whom she used to read) she made a will leaving money and directions that led to the founding of The Leeds Unmarried Women's Benevolent Institution two years later. Her last words were 'My work is done. Praise God for evermore.' She died in 1858, at the early age of thirty, and the headstone (now missing) on her grave in old St. Matthew's churchyard, while omitting her name, bore an eighteen line epitaph beginning 'Here lie the earthly remains of one who needs no lettered stone to tell her name and worth and state ...'.

Opposite Carr Manor stood a long since disused well provided by Joseph Oates (1743-1824). It was at the head of a small stream, and about sixty years ago the well cover was moved slightly to its present position because of building developments. It bears the inscription:

42. **Revolution Well**

Bog in the adjoining Field drain'd,
Spring open'd
& conducted hither,
For the benefit of the Passenger,
and the neighbouring House,
Nov! 5th 1788.
the 100th Anniversary from the land? of
KING WILLIAM
in memory of which happy Æra,
This is by Joseph Oates inscribed
the REVOLUTION WELL.

In the field almost opposite is a standing stone inscribed NEC SE COGNOSC^{T} TERRÆ VERT^{S} ANNIS. J. OATES. P. A.D. 1812. Fifty yards away is a hillock about four feet high and forty-feet across surrounded by bushes on which stand two trees. There is a tradition that it is a burial mound associated with the Civil War but there is no evidence to support this legend.

The highest point in Meanwood, which according to Ralph Thoresby may have had Roman associations, affords a very good view of Leeds and the countryside for miles around. Referred to as Tunnel Haw Hill in 1425 and as Tunninghall Hill in 1778, the spot is far better known as King Alfred's Castle. It was here in 1760 that Jeremiah Dixon built a folly which he dedicated to the memory of Alfred the Great. The ruin, which was demolished about forty years ago, bore the following inscription:

TO THE MEMORY OF
ALFRED THE GREAT
THE PIOUS AND MAGNANIMOUS
THE FRIEND OF
SCIENCE, VIRTUE, LAW AND LIBERTY
THIS MONUMENT
JEREMIAH DIXON OF ALLERTON
GLEDHOW CAUSED TO BE ERECTED
MDCCLX

*   *   *   *   *

These stories, some well documented but others passed down by word of mouth, have been culled from many sources and form part of the warp and weft of the community. The authors feel that it would be a shame for them to be lost for ever and so they are offered as a tail-piece to the Meanwood story.